TEACHER EDITION

GRACE FOR THE PACE

FINDING GOD'S STRENGTH
FOR YOUR DAILY RACE

PAUL CHAPPELL

Striving Together Publications
4020 E. Lancaster Blvd.
Lancaster, CA 93535
800.201.7748

Cover design by Andrew Jones
Layout by Craig Parker
Edited by Robert Byers, Rebekah Hanks, Tina Butterfield
Special thanks to our proofreaders.

ISBN 978-1-59894-097-8
Printed in the United States of America

Table of Contents

How to Use This Curriculum

Take a moment to familiarize yourself with the features of this *Striving Together* Sunday school curriculum:

Schedule

The lessons contained in this curriculum are undated, allowing you to begin and end the teaching series at any time. There are thirteen lessons that may be taught weekly any time of the year.

Student Edition Books

Companion books are available through *Striving Together Publications*. These contain:

- The outlines with blanks that students may fill in during the lessons

- Various Scripture quotations that are used throughout each lesson
- The introductory lesson overviews
- Study questions for review throughout the week
- A suggested memory verse for each lesson

These books are excellent tools for the members of a class. We suggest ordering enough books for each member of the class, plus additional copies for new members who enroll in the class throughout the teaching series. Giving class members a study book encourages faithfulness to the class, provides students with a devotional tool for use throughout the week, and allows them to review what they learned previously.

Text

The verses from which the lessons are taken are included at the beginning of each lesson. These are provided so that you may read them through several times in prayerful preparation for your time in class. Many teachers choose to memorize their key verses. During the class hour, we suggest that you use your own Bible for Scripture reading and encourage your class members to do so as well.

Overview and Lesson Aim

The overview and theme sections are provided so that you may be aware of the overall emphasis of each lesson, especially as they relate to the other lessons in the curriculum. These brief statements provide a snapshot of where each lesson will take the students.

Lesson Goals

Bible teaching has a higher goal than the delivery of information. That goal is a changed life. Students want to know what they are to do with what they are given from God's Word. As you prepare for and teach each lesson, emphasize how those listening may apply its truths throughout the week.

Teaching Outline

The abbreviated outline enables you to view the entire lesson at a glance to see how the content fits together. Teaching with an organized outline increases the students' abilities to understand and remember the lesson content.

A Renewing Grace

Text

MARK 16:1–11

1   And when the sabbath was past, Mary Magdalene, and Mary the mother of James, and Salome, had bought sweet spices, that they might come and anoint him.

2   And very early in the morning the first day of the week, they came unto the sepulchre at the rising of the sun.

3   And they said among themselves, Who shall roll us away the stone from the door of the sepulchre?

4   And when they looked, they saw that the stone was rolled away: for it was very great.

5   And entering into the sepulchre, they saw a young man sitting on the right side, clothed in a long white garment; and they were affrighted.

6   And he saith unto them, Be not affrighted: Ye seek Jesus of Nazareth, which was crucified: he is risen; he is not here: behold the place where they laid him.

7   But go your way, tell his disciples and Peter that he goeth before you into Galilee: there shall ye see him, as he said unto you.

8   And they went out quickly, and fled from the sepulchre; for they trembled and were amazed: neither said they any thing to any man; for they were afraid.

9   Now when Jesus was risen early the first day of the week, he appeared first to Mary Magdalene, out of whom he had cast seven devils.

10 *And she went and told them that had been with him, as they mourned and wept.*

11 *And they, when they had heard that he was alive, and had been seen of her, believed not.*

Overview

Grace has many facets: it provides our salvation, healing, hope, and purpose in life. We see grace illustrated vividly in the Resurrection. Grace transformed Mary's pain into hope, replaced the disciples' pessimism with faith, and gave their lives new purpose and meaning.

Many Christians have not yet come to understand the role grace plays in their daily walk with God, and as a result, they are living below their privileges as children of God. While the Resurrection is a true historical event, its impact is not exclusive to first century Christians; rather, God extends to today's Christian the grace to live a victorious Christian life through the power of Christ's Resurrection.

Lesson Aim

As Christians, we must understand the role of God's grace in renewing us to live and walk as regenerated creations in Christ. God gave us a constant reminder of His grace—the empty tomb.

Lesson Goals

At the conclusion of the lesson, each student should:
1. Understand the meaning of grace.
2. See the importance of the Resurrection.
3. Know how to deal with disappointment and unbelief.
4. Seek to fulfill God's purpose for life.
5. Be looking for opportunities to share the Good News with others.

Teaching Outline

I. Renewed from Pain
   A. Through salvation in Christ
   B. Through the Resurrection of Christ

II. Renewed from Pessimism
   A. Pessimism because of disappointment
   B. Pessimism because of unbelief

III. Renewed for a Purpose
   A. To share in the gift of His eternal life
   B. To share His Good News

A Renewing Grace

Text

MARK 16:1–11

1   And when the sabbath was past, Mary Magdalene, and Mary the mother of James, and Salome, had bought sweet spices, that they might come and anoint him.

2   And very early in the morning the first day of the week, they came unto the sepulchre at the rising of the sun.

3   And they said among themselves, Who shall roll us away the stone from the door of the sepulchre?

4   And when they looked, they saw that the stone was rolled away: for it was very great.

5   And entering into the sepulchre, they saw a young man sitting on the right side, clothed in a long white garment; and they were affrighted.

6   And he saith unto them, Be not affrighted: Ye seek Jesus of Nazareth, which was crucified: he is risen; he is not here: behold the place where they laid him.

7 But go your way, tell his disciples and Peter that he goeth before you into Galilee: there shall ye see him, as he said unto you.

8 And they went out quickly, and fled from the sepulchre; for they trembled and were amazed: neither said they any thing to any man; for they were afraid.

9 Now when Jesus was risen early the first day of the week, he appeared first to Mary Magdalene, out of whom he had cast seven devils.

10 And she went and told them that had been with him, as they mourned and wept.

11 And they, when they had heard that he was alive, and had been seen of her, believed not.

Introduction

Have you ever thought about how the disciples felt that first Easter morning? Everything they had believed in and hoped for seemed to be gone. The future that they had expected with Jesus, their dream of deliverance from Roman oppression, and the promise of a Comforter all seemed to be unmet expectations.

The disciples had not realized at first that the Cross and the tomb were part of God's plan—His means of bringing grace to lost and dying men and women. God's righteousness demands a penalty for sin, and His holiness forbids sin to enter Heaven. But the death, burial, and resurrection of Jesus Christ allow us to enjoy the full benefits of God's grace.

Paul put it this way in his epistle to the churches in Galatia: "Christ hath redeemed us from the curse of the law, being made a curse for us: for it is written, Cursed is every one that hangeth on a tree: That the blessing of Abraham might come on the Gentiles through Jesus Christ; that we might receive the promise of the Spirit through faith" (Galatians 3:13–14).

Sometimes we are tempted to take God's grace for granted. But as we study the renewal that grace brings into our lives, you will be reminded that grace changes everything.

Illustration

The song originally called "Faith's Review and Expectation" is better known by the name "Amazing Grace." It was written by the English slave trader John Newton who was a wicked and ungodly man until his life was changed forever by God's amazing grace. He became a preacher and worked for decades to end the slave trade. Such a transformation can only be explained by God's grace.

Newton referred to the day of his conversion, March 21, 1748, as "the great turning day." He wrote the words to his most famous song to accompany a sermon on 1 Chronicles 17:16–17, which he preached on New Year's Day in 1773. Newton's life is a lasting testimony to the power of grace (information taken from the John Newton Project at www.johnnewton.org).

Grace revealed itself to those at the empty tomb Easter morning and to those who met the risen Christ. But it is not just for them; grace is for every believer today. Through the story of the Resurrection, we will see how God's grace renewed the disciples and how that same grace is still renewing and transforming lives today.

I. Renewed from Pain

MARK 16:9

9 *Now when Jesus was risen early the first day of the week, he appeared first to Mary Magdalene, out of whom he had cast seven devils.*

Before Mary Magdalene met Jesus, her life was dark and demonic. Luke 8:2 describes her this way, *"And a certain woman, which had been healed of evil spirits and infirmities, Mary called Magdalene, out of whom went seven devils."* One demon would be bad enough, but seven evil spirits made her life of misery and pain a constant struggle. Everything changed for Mary when she met Jesus. For those who do not have a personal relationship with His grace, life is empty and unsatisfying.

Illustration

Cloaked in a long, black trench coat, 16-year-old Jeffrey Weise walked into the Red Lake High School in Red Lake, Minnesota on March 21, 2005, carrying two guns he had stolen from his grandfather after killing him in the family home. Weise killed a security guard, a teacher, and five students, and wounded seven others before killing himself.

Weise was obsessed with movies, video games, and music videos, especially those about murder and school shootings. He even created animations of murderous rampages, which he posted online. The devil is still busily working today, filling people's lives with pain and misery, lives which can only be renewed through God's grace.

Let's look at how grace changes our lives.

A. *Through salvation in Christ*
EPHESIANS 2:8
8   *For by grace are ye saved through faith; and that not of yourselves: it is the gift of God:*

Mary Magdalene was saved, not because she deserved salvation, but simply because of God's grace. On the day she was saved, the pain and suffering of her past was replaced with peace and freedom through grace.

PSALM 103:12
12 As far as the east is from the west, so far hath he removed our transgressions from us.

Grace removes the past. Many believers struggle with guilt over things that happened before they were saved. Mary's past could have weighed her down and kept her from serving God. God's grace removed her sin as far away as the east is from the west, and His grace will do the same for you. Jesus did not save Mary Magdalene only to leave her as she was; He saved her to give her a new, abundant life (John 10:10).

B. *Through the Resurrection of Christ*

Phillip Brooks, author of the Christmas carol "O Little Town of Bethlehem," also wrote these words:

> Tomb, thou shalt not hold Him longer;
> Death is strong, but Life is stronger;
> Stronger than the dark, the light;
> Stronger than the wrong, the right.
> Faith and Hope triumphant say,
> Christ will rise on Easter Day.

Mary was astonished and fearful after the crucifixion. Seeing the One who had transformed her life suffer such a horrific death on the Cross wasn't something she was prepared to see. Her grief was compounded when she came to the tomb to find her Lord's body missing. In Mark 16:6, the angel told her, *"He is risen."* Only experiencing the truth of the Resurrection could renew her heart and replace her pain with joy.

In *Confessions of a Grieving Christian*, Zig Ziglar wrote, "The longest twenty-four hours of my life were the hours after my daughter's death. I walked, praying and crying the whole way. But when I returned home, the Lord assured me through His Word, 'You will be fine; just keep walking, keep crying, and keep praying.'" The Resurrection gives us grace to overcome the pain and suffering of life. Some people seem to think that Christians should be exempt from pain, but this rationale is not what the Word of God teaches. Instead, the Bible says that God gives us grace that is sufficient for every need (2 Corinthians 12:9).

1 CORINTHIANS 15:19–20

19 *If in this life only we have hope in Christ, we are of all men most miserable.*

20 *But now is Christ risen from the dead, and become the firstfruits of them that slept.*

Without the Resurrection, there is no hope! The pain that is part of living in a fallen world can only be met and overcome through the grace of God. No matter how severe your pain is today, grace can bring you renewal and peace.

II. Renewed from Pessimism

MARK 16:11

11 *And they [the disciples], when they had heard that he was alive, and had been seen of her, believed not.*

The trials and pain of life can cause us to become skeptical, disappointed, and doubtful. When Mary told the disciples that Jesus was alive and that she had seen Him, they didn't believe her.

Pessimism abounds in America today. John Cleaver wrote, "The main emotion of the adult American who had all the advantages of wealth, education, and welfare is disappointment." Pessimism doesn't just spring up from nowhere; it is usually caused by one of two things.

A. Pessimism because of disappointment

The apostles were disappointed after the crucifixion. The dreams and plans they had anticipated with such eagerness—of ruling and reigning with Jesus Christ—had been dashed to pieces. They had expected Jesus to destroy Israel's enemies and set up His kingdom, but the arrest, trial, and death of Jesus left them feeling hopeless. Everything looked bleak. Even when hope was offered to them, they refused to accept it.

Has anyone ever let you down or disappointed you? Of course you have been disappointed. Disappointments can keep you from serving the Lord or from enjoying the good things in your life. Access the grace of God and rise above the pessimism that could limit your work for Him. President Dwight Eisenhower said, "Pessimism never won any battle."

B. Pessimism because of unbelief

The pessimistic disciples had been taught about the Resurrection; they just did not believe what Jesus had tried to reveal to them over and over again.

JOHN 14:3

3   And if I go and prepare a place for you, I will come again, and receive you unto myself; that where I am, there ye may be also.

MATTHEW 12:40

40   For as Jonas was three days and three nights in the whale's belly; so shall the Son of man be three days and three nights in the heart of the earth.

JOHN 2:19

19   Jesus answered and said unto them, Destroy this temple, and in three days I will raise it up.

Because they had not believed the teaching of Jesus, they doubted when things didn't work according to their plan. Unbelief and lack of faith makes us vulnerable to a pessimistic spirit. To strengthen your faith, go to the Bible. Romans 10:17 says, *"So then faith cometh by hearing, and hearing by the word of God."* You have nothing to lose, and everything to gain, by trusting in Jesus Christ. Remember that faith is not just a means to salvation; it is also to be the way we live the Christian life (2 Corinthians 5:7).

JOHN 20:18–20

18   Mary Magdalene came and told the disciples that she had seen the Lord, and that he had spoken these things unto her.

19   Then the same day at evening, being the first day of the week, when the doors were shut where the disciples were assembled for fear of the Jews, came Jesus and stood in the midst, and saith unto them, Peace be unto you.

20   And when he had so said, he shewed unto them his hands and his side. Then were the disciples glad, when they saw the Lord.

We live in a negative world. How easy it is to find ourselves surrounded by the "fraternity of discouragement." If we are not careful, we can adopt a pessimistic outlook without even realizing it. But Christians have no reason to be downcast. Jesus has already fought and won our battles for us, and the empty tomb is proof that the victory is ours.

Just as we are saved "by grace…through faith" we also overcome pessimism through the power of grace made real in our lives by faith. When the Syrians surrounded Elisha's house to capture him, his servant was afraid, but Elisha was confident (2 Kings 6:14–17). Why? Because faith let him see what God was doing behind the scenes.

> **TEACHING TIP**
>
> *Ask your students to identify areas in which they struggle with pessimism. Start the conversation by sharing an example from your own life. But be sure to also share how you overcame that pessimistic spirit. Don't leave the impression that it's okay to remain discouraged.*

Grace replaces our pessimism with hope. When the disciples realized that Jesus was alive again, their fear and uncertainty was replaced with gladness. Christians who are living with an awareness of God's grace will not be downcast and discouraged. Psalm 42:5 says, *"Why art thou cast down, O my soul? and why art thou disquieted within me? hope thou in God: for I shall yet praise him for the help of his countenance."* The Resurrection gives us grace to overcome disappointment and unbelief.

III. Renewed for a Purpose

MATTHEW 28:16–20

16 *Then the eleven disciples went away into Galilee, into a mountain where Jesus had appointed them.*

17 *And when they saw him, they worshipped him: but some doubted.*

18 *And Jesus came and spake unto them, saying, All power is given unto me in heaven and in earth.*

19 *Go ye therefore, and teach all nations, baptizing them in the name of the Father, and of the Son, and of the Holy Ghost:*

20 *Teaching them to observe all things whatsoever I have commanded you: and, lo, I am with you alway, even unto the end of the world. Amen.*

If ever a group of people were wandering and lacking in purpose, it was the disciples while Jesus was in the tomb. Everything they had been expecting was overthrown. Everything they had been trusting was shattered. They simply didn't know what to do next. So before He returned to Heaven, Jesus gave them a purpose and direction that would guide them the rest of their lives. It's what we call the Great Commission.

Maybe you are a little uncertain about your future and do not see a way out of trouble or confusion. Maybe you do not see how God might use your life for His service and His glory. God does have a plan and a purpose for your life. It is grace that applies resurrection power to help us reach that purpose. Here are two purposes God has for us.

A. To share in the gift of His eternal life

2 PETER 3:9

9 *The Lord is not slack concerning his promise, as some men count slackness; but is longsuffering to us-ward, not*

willing that any should perish, but that all should come to repentance.

1 Corinthians 15:3–4

3   For I delivered unto you first of all that which I also received, how that Christ died for our sins according to the scriptures;
4   And that he was buried, and that he rose again the third day according to the scriptures:

God does not want anyone to go to Hell. That's why He sent His Son to die for our sins on the Cross. Because our sins keep us from entering God's presence in Heaven, we must accept the sacrificial death of Christ to cleanse us from our sins. Accepting Christ's payment for our sins is the only way to be saved. Salvation not only places us in the family of God, it also gives us eternal life (John 3:16).

If you have never accepted the payment Jesus made for your sin, you do not have God's grace in your life. You have no hope of ever sharing in the gift of eternal life God designated for those who accept Christ as Saviour (Romans 6:23). I urge you to make that decision today and pray, "Lord, I know that I am a sinner and that You died and rose again for my sins. I ask You to come into my heart and be my Saviour. Amen."

God saves us, not only so we can have eternal life and grace for living, but also that we might touch the lives of others. All who have accepted the gift of eternal life have a great responsibility.

B. To share His Good News

John 20:21

21   Then said Jesus to them again, Peace be unto you: as my Father hath sent me, even so send I you.

God's purpose for our lives is to share with others the grace that saved us. Jesus illustrated that just as God had sent Him into the world, He was sending His followers—not just the original disciples, but every believer—to share the Good News.

Illustration

On the importance of sharing our faith, Charles Spurgeon once said, "If sinners will be damned, at least let them leap into Hell over our bodies. And if they will perish, let them perish with our arms about their knees, imploring them to stay. If Hell must be filled, let not one go there unwarned and unprayed for."

A man once said to me, "Pastor, it seems like everywhere I go, I meet someone from your church. They're going out into neighborhoods, passing out tracts, inviting people to church, and telling them how to be saved." That is what the church is supposed to do. Some places have turned the Great Commission into the Great Omission by failing to fulfill our responsibility to share the Good News.

A life lived for self is a miserable life. Joy comes from serving the Lord.

Conclusion

Grace changes everything. It transformed Mary Magdalene's pain to hope, the disciples' pessimism to faith, and every Christian's purposeless drifting to a lasting meaning in life. Without grace, we have no hope. With grace, all things are possible.

Grace renews us from the pains and hurts of our past, from the pessimistic doubt that threatens our present, and for God's divine purpose for our future. John Newton's hymn "Amazing Grace" includes these wonderful lines:

> The Lord has promised good to me
> His Word my soul secures
> He will my shield and portion be
> As long as life endures.

Study Questions

1. How did you come to realize that you needed God's grace in your life?
   Answers will vary.

2. Through what means does God's grace renew us from pain?
   Through salvation, through the Resurrection

3. How does the Resurrection give us hope for the future?
   Answers will vary.

4. Why do you think so many people are pessimists today?
   Because of disappointment, because of unbelief

5. In what areas are you tempted to doubt the promises of God?
   Answers will vary.

6. What are the purposes God has in offering you grace?
   To share His eternal life, to share His Good News

7. Whom do you know that needs to hear the Gospel?
   Answers will vary.

8. How can you demonstrate your appreciation for the grace of God?
   Answers will vary.

Memory Verses

EPHESIANS 2:4–5

4   But God, who is rich in mercy, for his great love wherewith he loved us,

5   Even when we were dead in sins, hath quickened us together with Christ, (by grace ye are saved;)

A Restoring Grace

Text

JOHN 18:25–27

25 And Simon Peter stood and warmed himself. They said therefore unto him, Art not thou also one of his disciples? He denied it, and said, I am not.

26 One of the servants of the high priest, being his kinsman whose ear Peter cut off, saith, Did not I see thee in the garden with him?

27 Peter then denied again: and immediately the cock crew.

Overview

Every child of God receives the Holy Spirit at the moment of salvation, and His full power and influence immediately become available to the believer. Though converted, Christians are not necessarily free from old patterns of worldly thoughts and actions. Sinful desires still remain.

If Christians are not careful, we can easily fall back into old habits, allowing those habits to take over and govern our actions and reactions. Fleshly patterns of decision-making always lead to consequences. When we sin, we need the restoring grace of God to bring us back into fellowship with Him. By properly responding to that grace, we will be renewed for His service.

Lesson Aim

We want to impress upon the student the importance of God's grace in rebuilding a strong relationship with Him and in restoring us to a position from which we can again effectively serve Him.

Lesson Goals

At the conclusion of the lesson, each student should:
1. Understand the common causes of failure to do right.
2. Discern the importance of a close relationship with God.
3. See how the process of restoration works.
4. Appreciate how much God loves us.
5. Respond to grace in order to be used in ministry and service by the Lord.

Teaching Outline

  I. Peter's Relapse
    A. He was proud.
       1. Peter thought he was stronger than others.
       2. Peter underestimated the persistence of Satan.
    B. He was prayerless.
    C. He was pretending.

  II. Peter's Restoration
    A. Jesus came to him.
    B. The Holy Spirit empowered him.

  III. Peter's Response
    A. Peter preached the truth of Christ.
    B. Peter proclaimed the work of Christ.

A Restoring Grace

Text

25 And Simon Peter stood and warmed himself. They said therefore unto him, Art not thou also one of his disciples? He denied it, and said, I am not.

26 One of the servants of the high priest, being his kinsman whose ear Peter cut off, saith, Did not I see thee in the garden with him?

27 Peter then denied again: and immediately the cock crew.

Introduction

The moment you were saved, you received the Holy Spirit of God. His presence in your life means that you have His power and influence available to you for every decision that you make and every action that you take. When we walk in the Spirit, we fulfill God's purposes for our lives, and we honor and please Him with what we do.

Our conversion, however, does not take away our old patterns of thinking and acting. If we are not careful, we can easily revert back to our old ways. The patterns of fleshly decision-making and behavior are traps that the devil uses to draw us away from following and serving God. The result is a tragic return to the failures of the past.

The Apostle Paul struggled with this scenario in his own life. He wrote, "*For we know that the law is spiritual: but I am carnal, sold under sin. For that which I do I allow not: for what I would, that do I not; but what I hate, that do I*" (Romans 7:14–15). What happens when we fail? What happens when we do that which we hate? Is there any hope? Yes!

The Lord does not discard us when we sin. Instead, He offers us His grace to restore us to fellowship and usefulness to Him. God's grace is essential not only for your salvation but also for your daily living in His service.

Illustration

If you have ever tried to lose weight, you know the pitfalls that accompany a diet. It's typically not a smooth process. We struggle, fail, and start over. Here are some helpful rules to remember if you are trying to shed a few pounds:

If no one sees you eat it, it has no calories.

If you drink a diet soda with a candy bar, the two cancel each other out.

When eating with someone else, you don't have to count the calories if you both eat the same thing.

Foods used for medicinal purposes, such as hot chocolate, toast, and Sara Lee cheesecake, NEVER count.

If you fatten up everyone else around you, you will look thinner.

Enjoy your diet!

When Peter fell back into his old behavior patterns of relying on his strong will and his instincts rather than on the power of the Lord, God did not abandon him. Instead, God extended grace to Peter to bring him back into a right relationship with Him and to prepare him for a life of service and ministry. That same process of relapse and restoration can happen to any of us. We're going to examine the things that the devil used to derail Peter; then we'll look at the way grace restored him; finally we'll see how he responded to grace.

I. Peter's Relapse

Peter began a life of faith and service when he responded to Jesus' call to leave his fishing boat and become a fisher of men. He had been an effective leader among the disciples and was part of the "inner circle," along with James and John. He spent three years in the presence of Jesus, listening to and learning from the Son of God. Yet none of those things kept Peter from falling back into his old ways of dealing with problems when the pressure was on. Three specific things caused Peter's relapse.

A. He was proud.

PROVERBS 16:18

18 Pride goeth before destruction, and an haughty spirit before a fall.

Peter had great talents and abilities but fell into the trap of self-reliance rather than God-reliance. He thought that, while others might be weak and need help, he could make it on his own.

Relying on our own strength and wisdom places us in great danger. Pride keeps us from receiving God's grace. First Peter 5:5 says, "...*God resisteth the proud, and giveth grace to the humble.*" Someone once said, "Pride is the disease that makes everyone sick except the one who has it." We see Peter's pride manifested in two particular areas.

1. PETER THOUGHT HE WAS STRONGER THAN OTHERS. JOHN 13:36–38

36 Simon Peter said unto him, Lord, whither goest thou? Jesus answered him, Whither I go, thou canst not follow me now; but thou shalt follow me afterwards.

37 Peter said unto him, Lord, why cannot I follow thee now? I will lay down my life for thy sake.

38 Jesus answered him, Wilt thou lay down thy life for my sake? Verily, verily, I say unto thee, The cock shall not crow, till thou hast denied me thrice.

Peter's mistake lay in evaluating his own devotion by comparing it to that of those around him. He believed that, even if others turned their backs on Jesus, he would remain faithful (Matthew 26:33). Everything we have—including our strength and dedication—is a gift from God (1 Corinthians 4:7). That realization should keep us from pride. We act foolishly when we compare ourselves to others (2 Corinthians 10:12).

Illustration

The CEO of a Fortune 500 company pulled into a service station to purchase gas. He went inside to pay, and when he came out, he noticed his wife engaged in a discussion with the service-station attendant. It turned out that she knew him. In fact, back in high school before she met her husband, she had dated him.

The CEO got in the car, and the two drove away in silence. He was feeling pretty good about himself when he finally spoke: "I bet I know what you're thinking. I bet you're thinking you're glad you married me, a Fortune 500 CEO, and not him, a service-station attendant."

"No," she replied. "I was thinking if I'd married him, he'd be a Fortune 500 CEO, and you'd be a service-station attendant."

2. PETER UNDERESTIMATED THE PERSISTENCE
OF SATAN.

LUKE 22:31–34

31 And the Lord said, Simon, Simon, behold, Satan hath desired to have you, that he may sift you as wheat:

32 But I have prayed for thee, that thy faith fail not: and when thou art converted, strengthen thy brethren.

33 And he said unto him, Lord, I am ready to go with thee, both into prison, and to death.

34 And he said, I tell thee, Peter, the cock shall not crow this day, before that thou shalt thrice deny that thou knowest me.

The devil does not try just once or twice to get us to sin. He returns again and again, probing our defenses, looking for a place of weakness. Peter was inspired to write later that the devil is like "a roaring lion" (1 Peter 5:8).

Live each day with the realization that there is a target on your back.

When Jesus overcame the temptation in the wilderness, the devil only left Him "for a season" (Luke 4:13). As long as you live, you remain a target for Satan's attacks. Do not let down your guard, even for one moment. A victory today does not guarantee victory tomorrow. Peter relapsed because he had a proud spirit, and as a result, he underestimated his enemy.

B. He was prayerless.

MATTHEW 26:34–36, 39–41

34 Jesus said unto him, Verily I say unto thee, That this night, before the cock crow, thou shalt deny me thrice.

35 Peter said unto him, Though I should die with thee, yet will I not deny thee. Likewise also said all the disciples.

36 Then cometh Jesus with them unto a place called Gethsemane, and saith unto the disciples, Sit ye here, while I go and pray yonder.

39 And he went a little farther, and fell on his face, and prayed, saying, O my Father, if it be possible, let this cup pass from me: nevertheless not as I will, but as thou wilt.

40 And he cometh unto the disciples, and findeth them asleep, and saith unto Peter, What, could ye not watch with me one hour?

41 Watch and pray, that ye enter not into temptation: the spirit indeed is willing, but the flesh is weak.

Pride precludes prayer, because prayer is based on reliance and dependence on God instead of self. Prayer is an assault on the autonomy of the human spirit. Though Jesus had just forewarned Peter that he would deny

Him, Peter was sleeping instead of praying for strength. Prayer is the means by which we obtain the power of God to fight and win our battles. Hymn writer William Cowper wrote:

Restraining prayer, we cease to fight;
Prayer makes the Christian's armour bright;
And Satan trembles when he sees
The weakest saint upon his knees.

Think of the contrast. Jesus, preparing for the coming ordeal of the Cross, urgently desired to pray. Peter, ignoring the coming temptation to deny Christ, urgently desired to sleep. He did not value prayer as a vital and essential resource to victory. Your flesh cannot withstand the attacks of the devil. The strength to triumph comes only through prayer.

C. He was pretending.

LUKE 22:54–62

54 Then took they him, and led him, and brought him into the high priest's house. And Peter followed afar off.

55 And when they had kindled a fire in the midst of the hall, and were set down together, Peter sat down among them.

56 But a certain maid beheld him as he sat by the fire, and earnestly looked upon him, and said, This man was also with him.

57 And he denied him, saying, Woman, I know him not.

58 And after a little while another saw him, and said, Thou art also of them. And Peter said, Man, I am not.

59 And about the space of one hour after another confidently affirmed, saying, Of a truth this fellow also was with him: for he is a Galilaean.

60 *And Peter said, Man, I know not what thou sayest. And immediately, while he yet spake, the cock crew.*
61 *And the Lord turned, and looked upon Peter. And Peter remembered the word of the Lord, how he had said unto him, Before the cock crow, thou shalt deny me thrice.*
62 *And Peter went out, and wept bitterly.*

Following Jesus "afar off" is a dangerous position. The only place for a Christian is close proximity to Jesus. We ought to always want to be in His presence. Peter, who only hours before had boasted of the depth of his commitment, was warming himself by the enemy's fire and denying he even knew Jesus.

Will you be the same Christian at work tomorrow that you are at church today? Will you be as committed to follow Him when you are challenged by others? Are you praying for strength or relying on your own power?

TEACHING TIP

Focus on the three problems that led to Peter's relapse. Discuss how pride leads to the other two problems. Pride blinds us to the need for prayer because we rely on ourselves rather than on God. Pride causes us to use a facade to keep others from seeing our true selves.

Have students share their own examples of how one or more of these problems has kept them from being used by God. Try to get as many people as possible involved in the conversation instead of just one or two.

II. Peter's Restoration

JOHN 21:3

3 Simon Peter saith unto them, I go a fishing. They say unto him, We also go with thee. They went forth, and entered into a ship immediately: and that night they caught nothing.

Every time we relapse, every time we fail, every time we choose to sin (never forget that we do not get to choose the consequences of that sin), God calls us back to Himself.

Peter knew he had let Jesus down, and he was embarrassed and ashamed. He went back to what he had known before—fishing. After allowing Peter to spend a frustrating night catching no fish, Jesus was standing on the shore, waiting for Peter.

A. *Jesus came to him.*

JOHN 21:12–17

12 Jesus saith unto them, Come and dine. And one of the disciples durst ask him, Who art thou? knowing that it was the Lord.

13 Jesus then cometh, and taketh bread, and giveth them, and fish likewise.

14 This is now the third time that Jesus shewed himself to his disciples, after that he was risen from the dead.

15 So when they had dined, Jesus saith to Simon Peter, Simon, son of Jonas, lovest thou me more than these? He saith unto him, Yea, Lord; thou knowest that I love thee. He saith unto him, Feed my lambs.

16 He saith to him again the second time, Simon, son of Jonas, lovest thou me? He saith unto him, Yea, Lord; thou knowest that I love thee. He saith unto him, Feed my sheep.

17 He saith unto him the third time, Simon, son of Jonas, lovest thou me? Peter was grieved because he said unto him the third time, Lovest thou me? And he said unto him, Lord, thou knowest all things; thou knowest that I love thee. Jesus saith unto him, Feed my sheep.

Though Peter had gone back to his old livelihood as a fisherman, Jesus did not give up on him. He knew that through the grace and power of the Holy Spirit, Peter had great potential. Even in chastisement, God will never stop loving you regardless of your failures.

When you are farther away from God than you should be, do not remain defeated, and do not forsake the call of God on your life. When Jesus dealt with Peter, He did not condemn Peter for denying Him or ask Peter why he had failed. He did not point out the folly of Peter's pride. Instead, He asked Peter about his love. Loving Jesus ensures we are having a right relationship with Him. Never forget to love Him; never forget how much He loves you.

Illustration

A lady from Korea told me the story of her life. Her father had been an American GI there during the war, but he was gone before she was born. Her mother tried to raise the little girl as best she could. For seven years she tried, until the difficulty was simply too much. She did something that is almost impossible for us to imagine—she abandoned her little girl to the streets.

This little girl was ruthlessly taunted by people who did not accept her because she was of mixed racial heritage. They called her the ugliest word in the Korean language, *tooki,* which means alien devil. It didn't take long for this little girl to draw conclusions about herself based on the way people treated her.

For two years she lived on the streets, until finally she made her way to an orphanage. At the orphanage, they told her about Jesus.

One day, word came that a couple from America was coming to adopt a little boy. All the children in the orphanage were excited because at least one little boy was going to have a better life.

The next day the couple came, and this is what the girl recalled: "It was like Goliath had come back to life. I saw the man with his huge hands lift up each and every baby. I knew he loved every one of them as if they were his own. I saw tears running down his face, and I knew that, if they could, they would have taken the whole lot home with them.

"He saw me out of the corner of his eye. I was nine years old, but I didn't even weigh thirty pounds. I was a scrawny thing. I had worms in my body. I had lice in my hair. I had boils all over me. I was full of scars. I was not a pretty sight. But the man came over to me, and he began rattling away something in English, and I looked up at him. Then he took this huge hand and laid it on my face. What was he saying? Later I found out that what he said was, 'I want this child. This is the child for me.' They took me back to America and raised me as their own child."

No matter what scars you bear in your life because you have gone away from God, He has chosen you. He reached down with grace to make you part of His family. That same love that led to your salvation, leads to your restoration when you fail. Just as Jesus came to Peter, He will come to you.

B. *The Holy Spirit empowered him.*

JOHN 14:16–17

16 And I will pray the Father, and he shall give you another Comforter, that he may abide with you for ever;

17 Even the Spirit of truth; whom the world cannot receive, because it seeth him not, neither knoweth him: but ye know him; for he dwelleth with you, and shall be in you.

ACTS 1:8

8 But ye shall receive power, after that the Holy Ghost is come upon you: and ye shall be witnesses unto me both in Jerusalem, and in all Judaea, and in Samaria, and unto the uttermost part of the earth.

It is a joy that we do not have to live the Christian life in our own strength. We would never make it. Instead, we have the power of the Holy Spirit dwelling inside us to fight and win our battles. There was nothing in Peter's past to suggest that he would become a powerful evangelist. Instead of training in seminary, he spent his days catching fish and had many rough edges. But when he was filled with the Spirit of God, his preaching produced incredible results. As a child of God, you have the same power living within you.

Illustration

A group of businessmen and church leaders met to decide on an evangelist who might come to speak in their city. They discussed inviting D.L. Moody. Speaker after speaker gave his impressions of the effectiveness of Moody's ministry. Finally, one man thought the praise was getting out of hand and spoke up. "You sound like D.L. Moody has a monopoly on God." "No," the answer came. "God has a monopoly on D.L. Moody."

As a young man, Moody was challenged with this statement: "It remains to be seen what God will do with a man who gives himself up wholly to Him." D.L. Moody said to himself, "Well, by God's grace, I will be that man." Yielding to God's power transforms our lives and ministries.

III. Peter's Response

How did Peter react to the love Jesus showed him? I have seen people over the years whom God had given second, third, or even fourth chances. Yet instead of responding by staying close to God, they drifted away again. Peter did not respond that way. Instead, he lived a life of service to God and others, feeding the sheep (1 Peter 5:2) just as Jesus had commanded.

A. Peter preached the truth of Christ.

ACTS 2:38–41

38 Then Peter said unto them, Repent, and be baptized every one of you in the name of Jesus Christ for the remission of sins, and ye shall receive the gift of the Holy Ghost.

39 For the promise is unto you, and to your children, and to all that are afar off, even as many as the Lord our God shall call.

40 And with many other words did he testify and exhort, saying, Save yourselves from this untoward generation.

41 Then they that gladly received his word were baptized: and the same day there were added unto them about three thousand souls.

On the Day of Pentecost there was much excitement. People were hearing the Gospel and responding. God's power was evident. And Peter was proudly proclaiming the name of Jesus that once he had denied. He was no longer embarrassed to be known as a Christian. Instead, he wanted to introduce others to the same grace that had restored him. One mark of a close relationship with Jesus Christ is the desire to introduce others to Him.

The message we carry is not one of our own strength or goodness but of the marvelous grace of God. The more we focus and meditate on what God has done for us, the more we want to tell others the Good News.

B. Peter proclaimed the work of Christ.

ACTS 4:8–12

8   Then Peter, filled with the Holy Ghost, said unto them, Ye rulers of the people, and elders of Israel,

9   If we this day be examined of the good deed done to the impotent man, by what means he is made whole;

10   Be it known unto you all, and to all the people of Israel, that by the name of Jesus Christ of Nazareth, whom ye crucified, whom God raised from the dead, even by him doth this man stand here before you whole.

11   This is the stone which was set at nought of you builders, which is become the head of the corner.

12   Neither is there salvation in any other: for there is none other name under heaven given among men, whereby we must be saved.

The message Peter had for those who heard him was of Christ's work of salvation. We are saved by grace through faith (Ephesians 2:8). There is no other way to God. There is no church, no leader, no work, no sacrifice, and no service that can earn you merit with God—it is all of grace.

The Christian life is more than simply being saved. God has a definite design for your life and predetermined purposes He wants you to fulfill.

Conclusion

There is more grace in God's heart than there is sin in your past. The restoring grace of Jesus is available to bring you back into fellowship with and service for Him. Like Peter, you may have failed. Maybe you have denied that you are a Christian to friends at work or to family members. Perhaps you have fallen back into old sinful habits. Maybe you have quit serving God or going to church.

Don't give up. Just as He did with Peter, Jesus will come to you. Even if you're in a stinking fishing boat surrounded by people who are just as withdrawn from God as you are, His grace is sufficient, and He loves you enough to reach down and lift you up. No matter what has happened, never forget His grace. In her hymn "He Giveth More Grace," Annie Flint wrote:

> His love has no limits, His grace has no measure,
> His power has no boundary known unto men;
> For out of His infinite riches in Jesus
> He giveth, and giveth, and giveth again.

Study Questions

1. What are some areas in which you return to fleshly patterns of behavior?
    Answers will vary.

2. What were the three causes of Peter's failure?
    Pride, prayerlessness, and pretending

3. How does pride manifest itself in your life?
    Answers will vary.

4. What took place that brought about Peter's restoration?
    Jesus came to him; the Holy Spirit empowered him.

5. What indicated the power of the Spirit was on Peter's life?
    He displayed effective preaching and witnessing; many people were converted.

6. How did Peter respond to his restoration?
    He preached the truth of Christ; he proclaimed the work of Christ.

7. What are some ways in which you are serving God today?
    Answers will vary.

8. How has God's grace restored your life?
    Answers will vary.

Memory Verses

JAMES 4:6–8

6 *But he giveth more grace. Wherefore he saith, God resisteth the proud, but giveth grace unto the humble.*

7 *Submit yourselves therefore to God. Resist the devil, and he will flee from you.*

8 *Draw nigh to God, and he will draw nigh to you. Cleanse your hands, ye sinners; and purify your hearts, ye double minded.*

A Replenishing Grace

Text

2 Timothy 2:1–3

1   Thou therefore, my son, be strong in the grace that is in Christ Jesus.

2   And the things that thou hast heard of me among many witnesses, the same commit thou to faithful men, who shall be able to teach others also.

3   Thou therefore endure hardness, as a good soldier of Jesus Christ.

Overview

Every Christian is living in the middle of a battlefield. Just as soldiers on the frontlines of war need time away for "R&R" (rest and recreation), we also need our strength replenished for the spiritual warfare we face. Our hectic lives sometimes make us feel like we're stuck in the spin cycle of a washing machine. That's where grace comes in.

Fighting the battle in our own strength is impossible. Spiritual muscles, like physical muscles, are only developed through effort and struggle. No one ever became a strong soldier for Christ without going through training. God's training program includes deploying His grace to help in preparing us to win the victory.

Lesson Aim

We want the student to understand how grace replenishes our strength for the battle and appreciate the vital role that suffering and struggles play as we mature spiritually.

Lesson Goals

At the conclusion of the lesson, each student should:

1. Know the role of grace in our spiritual battles.
2. Understand the purposes of suffering.
3. See the importance of a right attitude.
4. Guard against the doubt and discouragement that can sap our strength.
5. Value the forgiveness that comes to us through grace.

Teaching Outline

   I. His Grace Replenishes Our Strength
     A. Strength for service
     B. Strength for suffering
       1. When we are fearful
       2. When we are weary

  II. His Grace Replenishes Our Spirit
     A. From doubt to faith
     B. From discouragement to hope

 III. His Grace Replenishes Our Supply
     A. God supplies forgiveness by His grace.
     B. God supplies help by His grace.

A Replenishing Grace

Text

2 TIMOTHY 2:1–3

1 Thou therefore, my son, be strong in the grace that is in Christ Jesus.

2 And the things that thou hast heard of me among many witnesses, the same commit thou to faithful men, who shall be able to teach others also.

3 Thou therefore endure hardness, as a good soldier of Jesus Christ.

Introduction

Have you ever had "one of those days"? Have "those days" lasted for weeks at a time? Life in today's frenzied world can be very hectic.

Illustration

A little boy saw a commercial for a particular brand of detergent and went to the store to buy some. The grocer asked why he wanted the soap, and the boy explained that he wanted it to bathe his cat. The grocer said, "That soap is too strong for a cat. If you use it, you could kill him." The little boy bought the soap anyway. A few days later, the boy came back to the store, and the grocer asked, "How's your cat?" The boy said, "He died." The grocer replied, "I told you that would happen." The boy replied, "Oh, it wasn't the soap that got him, it was the spin cycle!"

If you're stuck in a spin cycle today, here's some good news: God's grace is more than sufficient for your needs.

Since the fall of man, we have lived in a world filled with pain, suffering, struggle, and death. We all need grace to replenish us as we walk through this world. One important role of the church—in addition to acting as a place of worship, service, and fellowship—is to provide a place where we can grow in the grace of the Lord. It's an island of hope and a haven of grace. Let's look at three ways God's grace replenishes us for the challenges of life.

I.   His Grace Replenishes Our Strength

Over the years, I've observed that when people get really busy with work, school, and other activities, frequently the first thing they cut is their service to God. They don't have time to teach Sunday school or work in the nursery or on the bus route any more. They remove those things from their schedule because they're just "too busy." But the work of the Lord is not optional—it is His design for our lives.

Paul wrote his last epistle, 2 Timothy, as he approached the end of his life. Timothy was Paul's son in the faith, and Paul served as his mentor when Timothy entered the ministry. Paul would no longer be there to help his young friend face the battles, struggles, opposition, and discouragement that would befall him. In fact, church history tells us that Timothy was martyred while pastoring the church at Ephesus. Because Timothy needed to grow in grace to effectively fulfill the ministry to which God had called him, the aged apostle wrote his valedictory letter to his young follower.

A. Strength for service
HEBREWS 12:28

28 Wherefore we receiving a kingdom which cannot be moved, let us have grace, whereby we may serve God acceptably with reverence and godly fear:

Paul did not tell Timothy he needed to "be all that he can be." He didn't write, "What your mind can conceive, you can achieve." This was not a self-help message. Our best will never be enough. Paul's message to Timothy was a message of utter dependence on God's grace. We need that same grace for our lives today. All the spiritual strength we possess is rooted in the grace of God.

Paul knew this truth first-hand. When he was struggling with his own weakness, he received this message from God: *"And he said unto me, My grace is sufficient for thee: for my strength is made perfect in weakness"* (2 Corinthians 12:9). Now he was sharing that truth with Timothy. To "be strong" means to "be enabled"—to have God's strength to do God's work. Grace gives us the ability to persevere when we have no more strength.

Illustration

A man wrote to missionary David Livingstone: "Mr. Livingstone, I am interested in joining you. Is there an easy way to get to where you are?" David Livingstone wrote back, "We are not looking for men who are looking for an easy way. We want men to join us who will make their own way if need be." Grace gives us strength to make a way where there is no way. We must have God's grace to serve Him acceptably (taken from *Building and Battling*, by Dr. Curtis Hutson).

B. Strength for suffering

JAMES 5:10

10 *Take, my brethren, the prophets, who have spoken in the name of the Lord, for an example of suffering affliction, and of patience.*

Some circles today propagate the notion that living for God results in health and prosperity. But the Bible says, *"All that will live godly in Christ Jesus shall suffer persecution"* (2 Timothy 3:12). Supreme Court Justice Antonin Scalia said, "Devout Christians are destined to be regarded as fools in modern society."

Grace gives us strength to resist outside pressures and to keep doing what is right. Grace does not deliver us from suffering; it sustains us in our suffering. God's grace sustains us through two particular times of suffering and keeps us from falling "by the way."

1. WHEN WE ARE FEARFUL

2 TIMOTHY 1:7

7   *For God hath not given us the spirit of fear; but of power, and of love, and of a sound mind.*

Sometimes our suffering makes us fearful. We wonder why sickness has come to our family or why we were laid off or why it was our child who got in trouble with the law. We are burdened by unexpected situations. We do not understand, and as a result, we dread what will happen next.

Someone said, "Worry pulls tomorrow's clouds over today's sunshine." I have watched some dear people endure almost unbelievable circumstances. Yet they had a strength—not their own, but one that comes from grace. The word *power* in 2 Timothy 1:7 is the Greek word *dunamis*, from which we get the word *dynamite*. We find great strength in the grace of God, and He gives this spirit to us freely and without reservation.

Illustration

For a number of years, our family has made a practice of spending some time during the holidays with those less fortunate than we are. It is a great way to keep children from focusing only on themselves. We've been to nursing homes and rescue missions, and one year, we went to the Antelope Valley Hospital to visit one of our church members who was very sick. We sang some of his favorite hymns and tried to encourage him. Though he was weak, he asked for his Bible so he could read us some of his favorite verses and share with us what God was teaching him. He was facing death, but God's Spirit gave him a dynamite faith that made him spiritually strong and unafraid.

2. WHEN WE ARE WEARY

2 CORINTHIANS 4:16

16 *For which cause we faint not; but though our outward man perish, yet the inward man is renewed day by day.*

The grace of God replenishes our strength when we are weary. The inward man is so much more important than the outward man, though our society communicates otherwise with its obsession of the physical body. You are more than the outward man; you are a living soul created by God for a purpose. His grace gives you the strength to keep going, no matter how tired you are.

Illustration

A father and son went shopping. As they walked through the store, the boy carried the shopping basket, and his dad placed the items in it. A lady came by, and seeing the load, she said, "Isn't that a big load for a little boy?" The boy replied, "Oh, don't worry about me. My dad knows how much I can carry!" God never gives you more than you can bear—if you rely on His grace for your strength.

The famous football coach Vince Lombardi told his team, "Fatigue makes cowards of us all." When you are weary, you will be tempted. It was no accident that the devil came to tempt Jesus when He was tired and weak after fasting for forty days. Jesus knew that God's grace was sufficient for Him, and it will be for you as well.

God's grace does more, however, than just replenish our strength.

II. His Grace Replenishes Our Spirit

Going through life's trials can be discouraging, and some Christians allow their spirits to be affected. Those who had been happy serving God are now downtrodden and negative. The greatest thing we can have in our homes and our churches is a spirit that is right with God. How is your spirit? Is your attitude toward God and His service bitter or cold?

Discouraged Christians allow their spirit to be scarred, maybe by other Christians who have let them down or leaders who have disappointed them. Maybe they don't trust people anymore—and their wounded spirits show. Trials come into everyone's life, but God wants to replenish you through His grace to help you overcome those obstacles rather than allow them to stop you from following Him.

A. From doubt to faith

PHILEMON 18–19, 25

18 *If he hath wronged thee, or oweth thee ought, put that on mine account;*

19 *I Paul have written it with mine own hand, I will repay it: albeit I do not say to thee how thou owest unto me even thine own self besides.*

25 *The grace of our Lord Jesus Christ be with your spirit. Amen.*

Onesimus, Philemon's slave, had run away to escape bondage and ended up in jail in Rome. There he met the Apostle Paul and became a Christian. Paul wanted him to return, but Philemon had lost faith in Onesimus and no longer trusted him. Paul wrote this short letter to Philemon, reminding him of the grace of God that led to his own conversion and that he (Paul) had led him to the Lord. He encouraged Philemon to accept Onesimus, just as God had accepted him.

49

How is that kind of forgiveness possible? How could Philemon replace his cynicism with a gracious spirit? Only God's grace can replenish our spirits as we yield our stubborn wills to Him and allow Him to love others through us. Paul concludes his letter by praying that God's grace would touch Philemon's spirit.

Though the Bible does not finish the story, church history tells us that Onesimus was accepted on his return; in fact, he eventually became the pastor of the church at Ephesus. Grace kept Philemon's spirit from reflecting hurts he had suffered, and it will do the same for you.

2 Timothy 4:22

22 *The Lord Jesus Christ be with thy spirit. Grace be with you. Amen.*

Many people talk about grace but don't exhibit it in their spirits. Grace can take you from doubt and questioning to faith, if you will seek God and find His grace to heal your wounded spirit.

> **TEACHING TIP**
>
> *Spend some time talking to your class about the dangers of doubting. Perhaps use the illustration of Thomas, who despite the testimony of the other disciples refused to believe that Jesus was alive. Why did Thomas refuse to believe? He had been hurt by the collapse of his dreams. He, like the others, had expected Jesus to overthrow the Romans and give the Jews their freedom. When Jesus died, Thomas did not want to believe again. Talk to your students about the hurts they have experienced, and show them how grace can overcome those hurts and rebuild their faith.*

B. *From discouragement to hope*

2 THESSALONIANS 2:16–17

16 *Now our Lord Jesus Christ himself, and God, even our Father, which hath loved us, and hath given us everlasting consolation and good hope through grace,*

17 *Comfort your hearts, and stablish you in every good word and work.*

By forgetting that God is working on our behalf, we find it easy to get discouraged when things become difficult. Grace gives us hope and comfort in the hard times and keeps us from giving up—Paul said it establishes us. Notice too how practical grace is. It is not just a feeling, it is the foundation for good words and good works.

Nothing shows God to the world more than demonstrating grace in difficult circumstances. When people see us living in hope instead of despair, they realize that we have something they do not. It's the same testimony Paul and Silas had that moved the Philippian jailer to ask them, *"What must I do to be saved?"* (Acts 16:30).

III. His Grace Replenishes Our Supply

Once kids grow to become teenagers, it is amazing how quickly a family's groceries can be consumed. The supplies just don't stretch very far, and a family with teenagers soon learns that they need to continue returning to the store to replenish the pantry. The same thing is true in the spiritual realm—we need to return to the throne of grace continually for our needs.

In the model prayer, Jesus taught us to pray, *"Give us this day our daily bread"* (Matthew 6:11). If God were to give us all the supply we would ever need, we would not need to return to Him. Instead, He gives us what we need for each day. Let's look at two essentials that God provides for us by His grace.

A. God supplies forgiveness by His grace.

EPHESIANS 2:8–9

8 For by grace are ye saved through faith; and that not of yourselves: it is the gift of God:

9 Not of works, lest any man should boast.

Our greatest needs are not economical, educational, or emotional. Our greatest need is God's forgiveness of our sin. Grace provides that forgiveness. Never forget that you were given grace because God is good and loving, not because you deserved it. Grace is unmerited, undeserved favor from God.

Only Jesus Christ can offer forgiveness because He is the one who paid the penalty for sin at Calvary. Religions around the world offer salvation in exchange for works, but there is no forgiveness apart from grace. We are not saved by anything we do; we are saved by grace through faith.

Illustration

Outside New York City lies a cemetery where a headstone bears a single word—"forgiven." There is no name, no dates of birth and death, no epitaph except the one-word testimony of a person who had found forgiveness.

Illustration

Many years ago, a little boy stood outside Buckingham Palace in London. He watched the banners waving in the breeze and the guards maintaining their posts. He wanted to go inside, but the guards wouldn't let him pass. The disappointed little boy was standing there crying when a man walked up and asked what was the matter. The boy replied, "I want to go into the palace and see the king." The man took his hand, walked the boy past the guards, and took him right into the throne room to see the king. That man had every right to take that boy into the presence of the king, for he was the Prince of Wales, and the king was his father.

B. God supplies help by His grace.

HEBREWS 4:15–16

15 *For we have not an high priest which cannot be touched with the feeling of our infirmities; but was in all points tempted like as we are, yet without sin.*

16 *Let us therefore come boldly unto the throne of grace, that we may obtain mercy, and find grace to help in time of need.*

Sometimes God calms the storm; other times He lets the storm rage and calms His child. Salvation meets our greatest need, but even after we are saved, we need God's grace *"to help in time of need."* Jesus is touched when we hurt. He suffered adversity and temptation as we do, and because He understands our pain, He wants to help and offers His grace freely.

Grace is the support beam for the soul after it has first received mercy. Grace is responsible for purifying the soul, upholding the spirit in all trials and difficulties, and enabling us to prove faithful unto death. Many people do not finish well; such failures are not failures of grace but rather a failure to come to God's throne to find the grace we need.

Illustration

I once heard the story of a boy who had a cocoon in a box in his room. When the moth began to break out of the cocoon, the boy noticed how it struggled. In an effort to help, he reached down and widened the opening of the cocoon freeing the moth. As the boy watched, he noticed that its wings remained shriveled. Something was wrong. The boy had not realized the struggle was necessary for the moth's muscles to develop. In his attempt to relieve the struggle, the boy had crippled the creature. Trials are necessary for spiritual growth, and God allows us to struggle so that we can grow and develop to be used for His glory.

Conclusion

God does not want us only to be saved; He also wants us to grow as believers and be strong in His grace. God's grace makes us strong enough to serve Him and to endure suffering. God's grace renews our spirit, replacing our doubt with faith and our discouragement with hope. And God's grace supplies forgiveness for our sins and help for our struggles.

Remember that the Christian life is not a life without trouble. Hymn writer Isaac Watts asked the question, "Must I be carried to the skies on flowery beds of ease?" The answer is no. But in every trial, in every trouble, in every tribulation, God provides sufficient grace—if we go to God and ask Him for it. Many times our first response is to complain to our friends or feel sorry for ourselves. Instead, we should make a beeline for the throne of grace, seeking the help He has promised to give.

Study Questions

1. In what ways do you find yourself involved in spiritual warfare?
Answers will vary.

2. In what two areas does God's grace give us strength?
Strength for service, strength for suffering

3. How has suffering helped you grow in your Christian life?
Answers will vary.

4. In what two areas does grace replenish our spirit?
From doubt to faith, from discouragement to hope

5. When has grace brought comfort to your life?
Answers will vary.

6. What does God provide for us through His grace?
Forgiveness, help

7. What are you doing to stay strong in spiritual warfare?
Answers will vary.

8. What struggle has God allowed in your life to make you stronger?
Answers will vary.

Memory Verses

HEBREWS 4:15–16

15 For we have not an high priest which cannot be touched with the feeling of our infirmities; but was in all points tempted like as we are, yet without sin.

16 Let us therefore come boldly unto the throne of grace, that we may obtain mercy, and find grace to help in time of need.

A Resting Grace

Text

1 Peter 5:10–12

10 But the God of all grace, who hath called us unto his eternal glory by Christ Jesus, after that ye have suffered a while, make you perfect, stablish, strengthen, settle you.

11 To him be glory and dominion for ever and ever. Amen.

12 By Silvanus, a faithful brother unto you, as I suppose, I have written briefly, exhorting, and testifying that this is the true grace of God wherein ye stand.

Overview

God designed the Christian life to move from grace to grace. We are saved by grace, but we also need sanctifying grace, serving grace, and sacrificing grace. Grace is especially important for times of suffering. In any difficulty, grace is a dependable foundation on which we can rest.

Grace strengthens and settles our faith so we can survive the storms of life. It is the source of our hope during trials, leading us to view the Word of God properly, as the foundation for our stability. God leads us through trials with the goal of building and strengthening our faith through His grace, and we must learn to view problems in light of this divine purpose.

Lesson Aim

We want the student to appreciate the role that grace plays in preparing us for the challenges of life, and understand how to appropriate that grace to enjoy the peace of God even through struggles.

Lesson Goals

At the conclusion of the lesson, each student should:

1. Grasp how God leads us from grace to grace.
2. See how grace helps us through suffering and affliction.
3. Learn the relationship between grace and faith.
4. Understand the importance of having a firm foundation for our faith.
5. View the Word of God as essential to success in the Christian life.

Teaching Outline

    I. Grace for Suffering
        A. Satanic attacks
        B. Personal afflictions

    II. Grace for Strengthening
        A. The completion of our faith
        B. The establishment of our faith
        C. The strengthening of our faith
            1. He has power to strengthen us.
            2. He has a purpose in strengthening us.

    III. Grace for Settling
        A. Settled on a foundation
            1. God's Word is our foundation.
            2. God's Word is our stabilization.
        B. Settled on a Person

A Resting Grace

Text

1 PETER 5:10–12

10   But the God of all grace, who hath called us unto his eternal glory by Christ Jesus, after that ye have suffered a while, make you perfect, stablish, strengthen, settle you.

11   To him be glory and dominion for ever and ever. Amen.

12   By Silvanus, a faithful brother unto you, as I suppose, I have written briefly, exhorting, and testifying that this is the true grace of God wherein ye stand.

Introduction

We live in a world characterized by worry and hurry. In contrast to the busyness and brokenness of the world around us, God's intention for His children is that they live in peace and rest. The key to living in His peace is found in His grace.

The solution to all problems is found not by living in denial but by living according to "the true grace of God."

We access more grace as we grow. God intends for us to grow from grace to grace, one step at a time, each step teaching us that in every trial and challenge peace and joy are available. Just as we are saved solely by God's grace, we grow and mature as believers, not through our strength or effort, but through the grace of God. Let's look now at the way grace helps us achieve spiritual rest even in a hectic world.

I. Grace for Suffering

During the most difficult times, grace is always available to us. Because of the evil that fills our world, opposition is ever-present. Some people do not understand or appreciate our commitment to follow God and the teachings of the Bible. Their main focus is not on our dedication to God but on their opposition to Him.

Grace helps us stand our ground when the opposition attacks. When a wicked world ridiculed Noah for building an ark though it had never rained before, how did he keep doing right? Genesis 6:8 tells us, *"But Noah found grace in the eyes of the LORD."* Noah was so close to God that God's favor meant more to him than man's favor. Never get over the fact that God has showered His grace on you, and never allow suffering or opposition to cause you to turn your back on God's grace.

A. Satanic attacks

JAMES 4:7

7   *Submit yourselves therefore to God. Resist the devil, and he will flee from you.*

60

We need grace to face Satanic opposition. There is a real devil who is active in our world, seeking people to devour and destroy. He does not want you to glorify God with your life or to grow in grace. He promises the best, but he pays the worst. He promises honor, but pays with disgrace. He promises pleasure, but pays with pain. He promises profit, but pays with loss. He promises life, but pays with death. He is a liar.

2 CORINTHIANS 12:7–9

7   And lest I should be exalted above measure through the abundance of the revelations, there was given to me a thorn in the flesh, the messenger of Satan to buffet me, lest I should be exalted above measure.

8   For this thing I besought the Lord thrice, that it might depart from me.

9   And he said unto me, My grace is sufficient for thee: for my strength is made perfect in weakness. Most gladly therefore will I rather glory in my infirmities, that the power of Christ may rest upon me.

God allowed Satan to attack the Apostle Paul. I believe this attack took the form of a physical infirmity. Paul asked for healing from God, but he did not receive it. Some people teach that you are not right with God if you are not in perfect health, but verse nine clearly teaches that it is not always God's will to heal His children. Paul was suffering that he might have a Christ-like humility that God could bless.

Often our focus is on getting God to remove the thorn when instead He intends to improve us. God used Paul's thorn in the flesh to teach him about the power and importance of grace and to keep him from being lifted up in pride. Someone once said, "Rather than ask for a lighter load, ask for a stronger back." Grace will help you overcome the attacks of the evil one through the power of Christ.

B. *Personal afflictions*

The afflictions you experience happen to others as well. Bad things do happen to good people. Although Job was a mature and godly believer (Job 1:1), his exemplary life did not isolate him from suffering physical, emotional, and spiritual pain.

1 CORINTHIANS 10:13

13 *There hath no temptation taken you but such as is common to man: but God is faithful, who will not suffer you to be tempted above that ye are able; but will with the temptation also make a way to escape, that ye may be able to bear it.*

1 PETER 1:6–7

6 *Wherein ye greatly rejoice, though now for a season, if need be, ye are in heaviness through manifold temptations:*
7 *That the trial of your faith, being much more precious than of gold that perisheth, though it be tried with fire, might be found unto praise and honour and glory at the appearing of Jesus Christ:*

When our hearts are aching and things are not going well, we have a choice. We can allow problems to draw us closer to God or drive us away from Him.

Illustration

In her book *The Hiding Place*, Corrie ten Boom told of her imprisonment at the dreaded Nazi death camp Ravensbruck. When she and her sister Bettie were placed in an overcrowded barrack infested with fleas, Corrie complained, but Bettie recognized that they should give thanks for everything. Corrie retorted, "There's no way even God could make me thankful for a flea." Later they found that theirs was the only barrack in the camp the guards would not enter—because of the fleas! They were able to hide the Bible they had smuggled in and hold Bible studies with the other prisoners, safe from the guards, thanks to God's provision of fleas. God always has a reason for everything that happens in our lives.

II. Grace for Strengthening

Scripture repeatedly contrasts our strength and God's strength. Every time we rely on our strength, we fail; every time we rely on God's strength, we succeed. Just as we go to a gym to strengthen our physical muscles, we need to work our spiritual muscles and increase our faith through God's grace. Let's look at the relationship between His grace and our faith.

A. The completion of our faith

When Peter prays for God to *"make you perfect"* (verse 10) what does he mean? Does perfection mean that we will be without sin? No. Rather, when the Bible uses the term *perfect*, the meaning is completeness—lacking nothing. Is your faith complete yet, or are you still growing as a Christian?

Illustration

In the *Last Days Newsletter*, Leonard Ravenhill tells about a group of tourists visiting a picturesque European village. Having seen the castles and cathedrals of Europe, they weren't very impressed with the village. In a rather patronizing way, one tourist asked an old man seated by a fence, "Were any great men born in this village?" The old man replied, "Nope, only babies." No one is born spiritually strong. We have to grow in grace to achieve what God has in store for us.

The faith you received at salvation is not sufficient to take you all the way through your life. Your faith needs to grow and develop. Some people never do mature as believers. Though they have been saved for years, they do not demonstrate any greater obedience or love to God than they had at the beginning. Salvation is the miracle of a moment, but Christian maturity is the work of a lifetime.

B. The establishment of our faith

2 THESSALONIANS 2:16–17

16 Now our Lord Jesus Christ himself, and God, even our Father, which hath loved us, and hath given us everlasting consolation and good hope through grace,

17 Comfort your hearts, and stablish you in every good word and work.

God wants our faith to be certain and sure. David said, *"My heart is fixed, O God, my heart is fixed: I will sing and give praise"* (Psalm 57:7). The church today needs established Christians to exhibit the characteristics of mature faith—Christians who are not fickle in their commitments but are solid and dependable.

When our faith is not established, our prayers will not be answered (James 1:7), and we will be unstable (James 1:8). If we are unstable and our prayers unanswered, we will begin to drift away from God. Grace grounds and establishes our faith.

C. The strengthening of our faith

What does it mean to have strong faith? A strong faith is one that cannot be shaken by circumstances because it is focused on God. It is the faith of Noah who built an ark though he had never seen rain. It is the faith of Abraham who believed he would have a son though he was one hundred years old. It is the faith of Joshua who saw the walls of Jericho fall down flat, though all odds were against him.

1. HE HAS POWER TO STRENGTHEN US.
PHILIPPIANS 4:13
13   *I can do all things through Christ which strengtheneth me.*

It is our duty to grow strong in our faith. God strengthens our faith through His grace. His purpose in that strengthening is not that we may boast or be recognized by others but that we may accomplish the good works He has planned for us to fulfill (Ephesians 2:10).

2. HE HAS A PURPOSE IN STRENGTHENING US.
LUKE 22:32
32   *But I have prayed for thee, that thy faith fail not: and when thou art converted, strengthen thy brethren.*

Jesus' purpose was for Peter's faith to be a source of strength and encouragement to the other disciples after his repentance. We become mature believers and gain strong faith not to benefit ourselves, but to have a positive impact on others. We are strengthened for service to Him and for Him.

III. Grace for Settling

Peter also talked about our being settled (verse 10). We live in a very mobile society. People are constantly moving from place to place, job to job, even church to church. Most people are unsettled, not just physically, but spiritually. There is *"a rest to the people of God"* (Hebrews 4:9) that is available to God's children. For us to be settled, we need to build our lives on something solid.

A. Settled on a foundation

No structure is stronger than the foundation on which it is built. Living in California, we know a lot about earthquakes. Buildings are built to very strict codes to ensure that they can last even if the ground moves. Every time we build a new building, the crew starts by digging. The bigger the building will be, the deeper the foundation must go. When your life is unsettled, you need a firm foundation.

1. GOD'S WORD IS OUR FOUNDATION.

MATTHEW 7:24–27

24 *Therefore whosoever heareth these sayings of mine, and doeth them, I will liken him unto a wise man, which built his house upon a rock:*

25 *And the rain descended, and the floods came, and the winds blew, and beat upon that house; and it fell not: for it was founded upon a rock.*

26 *And every one that heareth these sayings of mine, and doeth them not, shall be likened unto a foolish man, which built his house upon the sand:*

27 *And the rain descended, and the floods came, and the winds blew, and beat upon that house; and it fell: and great was the fall of it.*

Illustration

Construction on the Leaning Tower of Pisa, one of the world's most famous landmarks, began in 1173. But the foundation for the 185-foot tall tower was only ten feet deep. To compound that problem, the marshy, unstable soil of the area (the word *pisa* means "marshy land"!) began to shift under the weight of the tower even before construction was completed. Without massive engineering work from the 1960s to the 1990s, including counter balancing, constructing anchor lines, and reshaping the ground around the tower, it would have collapsed. In the same way, unless our lives are built on a solid foundation, they will not be able to stand.

God gives us the Bible—every single word—as a foundation, the only sure foundation for our lives. We do not need to base our actions on opinions or philosophies but on the Word of God. Why do we go to church? Because the Bible says to go. Why do we tithe? Because the

Bible says to tithe. Why do we go soulwinning? Because the Bible says to win souls. Why do we dress modestly? Because the Bible says to do so. Many believers today are so spiritually illiterate that they do not recognize what the normal Christian life is supposed to look like. Make sure your life is built on the unchanging Word of God.

2. GOD'S WORD IS OUR STABILIZATION.

EPHESIANS 4:11–15

11 *And he gave some, apostles; and some, prophets; and some, evangelists; and some, pastors and teachers;*

12 *For the perfecting of the saints, for the work of the ministry, for the edifying of the body of Christ:*

13 *Till we all come in the unity of the faith, and of the knowledge of the Son of God, unto a perfect man, unto the measure of the stature of the fulness of Christ:*

14 *That we henceforth be no more children, tossed to and fro, and carried about with every wind of doctrine by the sleight of men, and cunning craftiness, whereby they lie in wait to deceive;*

15 *But speaking the truth in love, may grow up into him in all things, which is the head, even Christ:*

Notice again in this passage the emphasis on service. The pastor and evangelist are not the only ones who do the work; the saints are to minister as well. Our service is effective only if we are stable ourselves. God does not want us to be uncertain and unsettled, tossed around by every breeze. A child learning to walk falls down when confronted by any obstacle. He is easily moved. If you have not grown in your faith since salvation, no matter your age, you are still a spiritual baby, immature and unstable. The Bible gives stability to our lives so we can live as God intends us to live.

B. Settled on a Person

1 CORINTHIANS 3:11

11 *For other foundation can no man lay than that is laid, which is Jesus Christ.*

Comparing himself to a builder, the Apostle Paul told the Corinthians that no foundation, other than our relationship with Jesus, can serve as the basis for a godly life. Membership in a church, catechism, baptism, or confession does not substitute for a relationship with the Lord Jesus Christ. That relationship is the only foundation for life.

MATTHEW 16:17–18

17 *And Jesus answered and said unto him, Blessed art thou, Simon Barjona: for flesh and blood hath not revealed it unto thee, but my Father which is in heaven.*
18 *And I say also unto thee, That thou art Peter, and upon this rock I will build my church; and the gates of hell shall not prevail against it.*

Jesus is the rock that is never shaken or moved. If you build your life on your relationship with Him, you have the basis for a settled and successful life. Without Him, you have no hope. Make sure that your life is built on Jesus Christ. Jesus told Peter that He would build His church on the rock—the rock meaning Him, the Son of God, not Peter (as some erroneously teach). Jesus is "the church's one foundation." Peter was a little rock; Jesus is a mountain. The church is not built on a man but on the finished work of our Saviour.

1 CORINTHIANS 10:4

4 *And did all drink the same spiritual drink: for they drank of that spiritual Rock that followed them: and that Rock was Christ.*

Conclusion

Grace provides a place of rest in a hectic and unsettled world. Grace provides help in times of suffering. Grace provides strength for our faith. And grace provides a sure and settled foundation for our lives. The question is this: are you resting and settled in God's grace today?

Edward Mote, a Baptist pastor in England in the late 1800s wrote these words in his hymn "The Solid Rock."

My hope is built on nothing less
Than Jesus' blood and righteousness;
I dare not trust the sweetest frame,
But wholly lean on Jesus' name.

When darkness veils His lovely face,
I rest on His unchanging grace;
In every high and stormy gale,
My anchor holds within the veil.

His oath, His covenant, His blood
Support me in the whelming flood;
When all around my soul gives way,
He then is all my hope and stay.

When He shall come with trumpet sound,
Oh, may I then in Him be found;
Dressed in His righteousness alone,
Faultless to stand before the throne.

Refrain
On Christ, the solid Rock, I stand;
All other ground is sinking sand,
All other ground is sinking sand.

Study Questions

1. In what two types of suffering does grace help us?
   Satanic attacks, personal affliction

2. How has grace helped you deal with affliction in your life?
   Answers will vary.

3. In what three ways does grace help our faith?
   Completes our faith, establishes our faith, strengthens our faith

4. What two truths did we learn about God's strengthening of our faith?
   He has the power to strengthen; He has a purpose for strengthening.

5. In what ways is your faith stronger now than it was when you were saved?
   Answers will vary.

6. How does grace settle us as believers?
   Settled on a foundation, settled on a Person

7. What two things does the Bible provide for our faith?
   Foundation, stability

8. When have you used a verse or passage from the Bible to keep you on track?
   Answers will vary.

Memory Verses

2 CORINTHIANS 12:7–9

7   And lest I should be exalted above measure through the abundance of the revelations, there was given to me a thorn in the flesh, the messenger of Satan to buffet me, lest I should be exalted above measure.

8   For this thing I besought the Lord thrice, that it might depart from me.

9   And he said unto me, My grace is sufficient for thee: for my strength is made perfect in weakness. Most gladly therefore will I rather glory in my infirmities, that the power of Christ may rest upon me.

A Redeeming Grace

Text

EPHESIANS 2:1–9

1   And you hath he quickened, who were dead in trespasses and sins;

2   Wherein in time past ye walked according to the course of this world, according to the prince of the power of the air, the spirit that now worketh in the children of disobedience:

3   Among whom also we all had our conversation in times past in the lusts of our flesh, fulfilling the desires of the flesh and of the mind; and were by nature the children of wrath, even as others.

4   But God, who is rich in mercy, for his great love wherewith he loved us,

5   Even when we were dead in sins, hath quickened us together with Christ, (by grace ye are saved;)

6   And hath raised us up together, and made us sit together in heavenly places in Christ Jesus:

7   That in the ages to come he might shew the exceeding riches of his grace in his kindness toward us through Christ Jesus.

8   For by grace are ye saved through faith; and that not of yourselves: it is the gift of God:

9   Not of works, lest any man should boast.

Overview

God has a heart of grace and love for every one of us. If He did not, we would all be in Hell, which is what we deserve.

But grace provides the means for our salvation and a way to join God in Heaven for eternity.

Often, when people have been saved for a number of years, they take that grace for granted and lose their appreciation for it. In this lesson, we will look at the glory of God's grace and focus on how much that grace cost Jesus Christ. Then we'll look at the power of His grace, and finally we'll see how we can partake of the riches of grace that are freely offered to us.

Lesson Aim

We want the student to gain a new appreciation for the great gift of salvation and understand how to apply the grace that purchased salvation to their own lives and their interactions with others.

Lesson Goals

At the conclusion of the lesson, each student should:

1. Be filled with gratitude for the wonderful gift of salvation.
2. Fully understand the cost of our redemption.
3. Grasp the power of God's grace for holy living.
4. Know how we can be partakers of God's grace.
5. Have a renewed vision to share His grace with others.

Teaching Outline

I. The Payment of Grace
   A. A payment of Christ's love
   B. A payment of Christ's blood

II. The Power of Grace
   A. Power to redeem us

    B.   Power to reclaim us

    C.   Power to renew us

III. The Partaking of Grace

    A.   By faith in Christ's work

    B.   By faith in Christ's work alone

A Redeeming Grace

Text

EPHESIANS 2:1–9

1 And you hath he quickened, who were dead in trespasses and sins;

2 Wherein in time past ye walked according to the course of this world, according to the prince of the power of the air, the spirit that now worketh in the children of disobedience:

3 Among whom also we all had our conversation in times past in the lusts of our flesh, fulfilling the desires of the flesh and of the mind; and were by nature the children of wrath, even as others.

4 But God, who is rich in mercy, for his great love wherewith he loved us,

5 Even when we were dead in sins, hath quickened us together with Christ, (by grace ye are saved;)

6 And hath raised us up together, and made us sit together in heavenly places in Christ Jesus:

7   That in the ages to come he might shew the exceeding riches of his grace in his kindness toward us through Christ Jesus.
8   For by grace are ye saved through faith; and that not of yourselves: it is the gift of God:
9   Not of works, lest any man should boast.

Introduction

God has a heart of love and grace for us, not because of who we are, but because of who He is. It is His nature and His character not only to love but also to demonstrate that love. His love for us is the driving force behind the life, death, and resurrection of Jesus Christ. That it is the very nature of God to love His creations is the reason we receive grace, for there is nothing lovely in us.

Often we are tempted, especially if we have been saved for a number of years, to take God's grace for granted rather than appreciate it for the wonderful gift it is. In this lesson, we are going to look at how much grace cost God. Then we'll look at the power of His grace and finally at the way we can partake of that grace. Grace is too great a gift to hoard. There are three facets of grace we need to understand in order to truly know God.

I.   The Payment of Grace

EPHESIANS 2:4–5
4   But God, who is rich in mercy, for his great love wherewith he loved us,
5   Even when we were dead in sins, hath quickened us together with Christ, (by grace ye are saved;)

Grace is free. We cannot earn it or pay for it in any way. Yet while it is free to us, Jesus Christ paid an exorbitant price. He laid down His life as payment, making it possible for us to receive the grace of God. There is only one explanation for such a sacrifice—love.

A. A payment of Christ's love

JOHN 3:16

16 For God so loved the world, that he gave his only begotten Son, that whosoever believeth in him should not perish, but have everlasting life.

Before you were born, God knew you and loved you. Love is His nature; it is who He is (1 John 4:8). That love explains why Christ died for us. He became a willing sacrifice so we could receive His grace.

Illustration

One day when Billy Graham was driving through a small southern town, he was stopped by a policeman and charged with speeding. Though Graham admitted his guilt, the officer told him that he would have to appear in court. In the courtroom, the judge asked, "Guilty, or not guilty?" When Graham pleaded guilty, the judge replied, "That'll be ten dollars—one dollar for every mile you were going over the limit." At that point, the judge recognized the famous minister. "You have violated the law," he said. "The fine must be paid, but I am going to pay it for you." He took a ten-dollar bill from his own wallet, attached it to the ticket, and then took Graham out and bought him a steak. That is how God treats a repentant sinner. That is what grace does for us.

Romans 5:8
8   But God commendeth his love toward us, in that, while we were yet sinners, Christ died for us.

Knowing that we are sinners who fall short of His glory and perfection, God loves us anyway. The Bible concept of sin is to miss the mark, to fail to reach the holiness God demands. And though God loves us, our sin separates us from Him because nothing short of perfection can come into His presence. Our sin is why the payment of Christ's love was required.

B. A payment of Christ's blood

1 Peter 1:18–19
18   Forasmuch as ye know that ye were not redeemed with corruptible things, as silver and gold, from your vain conversation received by tradition from your fathers;
19   But with the precious blood of Christ, as of a lamb without blemish and without spot:

Jesus not only said He loved us, but He voluntarily went to the Cross of Calvary and shed His blood for our salvation. The blood of lambs had been offered by the Israelites for hundreds of years as a symbol of the blood the Lamb of God would one day shed. But the blood of animals could only symbolize forgiveness; it could not take sins away (Hebrews 10:1–4). Nothing less than the perfect, precious blood of God's Son could serve as the atonement for sin that would afford us forgiveness and grace.

Romans 3:23–25
23   For all have sinned, and come short of the glory of God;
24   Being justified freely by his grace through the redemption that is in Christ Jesus:

25   *Whom God hath set forth to be a propitiation through faith in his blood, to declare his righteousness for the remission of sins that are past, through the forbearance of God;*

The word *propitiation* means "a satisfactory payment" which is the blood of Christ which covers our sin. Only the blood of a perfectly sinless Saviour can take away the penalty of sin. Jesus came into the world for the purpose of shedding His blood so that you could have God's grace. Never forget the price that was paid for your salvation.

II. The Power of Grace

EPHESIANS 2:8

8 For by grace are ye saved through faith; and that not of yourselves: it is the gift of God:

The power of grace has a miraculous impact on our relationship with God. We do not always appreciate that power because we fail to grasp the enormity of our sin in God's eyes. He hates sin with a fierce anger, and because of our sin, He had to condemn the creation He loves to eternal separation from Him in the torments of Hell (John 3:18–19). But grace bridges that immense gulf between God and us, allowing wretched sinners into His holy presence. We do not deserve Heaven or forgiveness of sins, but we receive both by grace when we are saved.

A. Power to redeem us

ROMANS 3:24

24 Being justified freely by his grace through the redemption that is in Christ Jesus:

81

What does it mean to be saved? To be saved is to be forgiven of sin, redeemed by the blood of Christ. Redemption is the release that follows the payment of a ransom. None of us could ever pay the debt we owe for our sin, but God offers salvation because He is not willing that any should perish (2 Peter 3:9).

EPHESIANS 1:7

7 *In whom we have redemption through his blood, the forgiveness of sins, according to the riches of his grace;*

The forgiveness we have received is a measure of *"the riches of his grace."* Such an extravagant gift can be given only by Someone with unlimited resources. Because the blood of Jesus is eternal and incorruptible, it is sufficient as a payment for the sin of everyone who accepts Him as Saviour by faith. We cannot redeem ourselves, but He can.

Illustration

A man dies and goes to Heaven. St. Peter meets him at the pearly gates. (That's not a Bible truth, but this story does illustrate grace.) St. Peter says, "Here's how it works. You need one hundred points to make it into Heaven. You tell me all the good things you've done, and I give you a certain number of points for each item, depending on how good it is. When you reach one hundred points, you get in."

"Okay," the man says, "I was married to the same woman for fifty years and never cheated on her, even in my heart." "That's wonderful," says St. Peter, "that's worth three points!" "Three points?" he says. "Well, I attended church all my life and supported its ministry with my money and service." "Terrific!" says St. Peter, "that's certainly worth a point." "One point? How about this: I started a soup kitchen in my city and worked in a shelter for homeless veterans." "Fantastic, that's good for two more points," Peter says. "TWO POINTS!" the man cries, "At this rate, the only way I will get into Heaven is by the grace of God!" "Come on in!" Peter says. The only way any of us will ever get in to Heaven is by grace alone.

B. Power to reclaim us

ROMANS 3:24–25

24 Being justified freely by his grace through the redemption that is in Christ Jesus:

25 Whom God hath set forth to be a propitiation through faith in his blood, to declare his righteousness for the remission of sins that are past, through the forbearance of God;

When we are saved, God declares the righteousness—the perfect holiness—of Jesus Christ to be ours. He makes us righteous through the sacrifice of Christ, and He places us in His family. We must remember that, even though God loves us, He would not be righteous Himself if He overlooked our sin. For Him to remain righteous while forgiving us, Jesus had to satisfy God's holy demands for justice so that our sins could be taken away. He satisfied this demand by His sacrifice. Although we were dead in sin, grace reclaimed us, made us righteous, and gives us a new life in Christ.

Illustration

In December of 1967, Dr. Christiaan Barnard of South Africa performed the first successful human heart transplant. Hoping to extend his life, the patient, a 54-year-old man suffering from incurable heart disease, was willing to assume the risks of undergoing the first transplant. Though the operation was a success, the patient died eighteen days later from pneumonia. Dr. Barnard was a gifted medical doctor and pioneer in the field of organ transplants, but he could not give lasting life to his patients. When God gives us a new heart at salvation, it provides eternal life, not a short-term fix.

C. Power to renew us

TITUS 2:11–13

11 For the grace of God that bringeth salvation hath appeared to all men,

12 Teaching us that, denying ungodliness and worldly lusts, we should live soberly, righteously, and godly, in this present world;

13 Looking for that blessed hope, and the glorious appearing of the great God and our Saviour Jesus Christ;

God's grace changes us from the inside out. It changes what we want and how we live. Grace is not just about giving us eternal life; it also works in our lives to conform us to the image of God's Son (Romans 8:29). You can never produce the fruit of the Spirit on your own; only through grace can we bear fruit.

Some people turn grace into a license to live as they choose. Throwing off constraints is not grace. Grace is the inner working of God's Spirit that teaches us to turn away from the temptations of the world and live soberly as we look for Christ's triumphant return. Using grace as an excuse to live wickedly makes a mockery of one of the most precious gifts God has given to us.

> **TEACHING TIP**
>
> *Go through the list in Titus 2:11–13 and contrast the
> things that grace teaches us to avoid with the things
> grace teaches us to follow. It's crucial to help the students
> understand the purpose of grace to counteract the false
> teaching that permeates so many churches today. Focus
> on these points: 1) grace denies lust and worldliness; 2)
> grace teaches righteous living; and 3) grace teaches us to
> focus on Jesus and His return for His children.*

III. The Partaking of Grace

EPHESIANS 2:8–9

8   For by grace are ye saved through faith; and that not of
yourselves: it is the gift of God:
9   Not of works, lest any man should boast.

The Bible tells us that grace is offered to everyone, but
not everyone receives this gift. How can God's grace become
a reality in our lives? How can we access that power to receive
salvation and to equip us for a life of service? How can we
be certain that we are saved from sin and that Heaven is our
eternal home?

A. By faith in Christ's work

TITUS 3:4–7

4   But after that the kindness and love of God our Saviour
toward man appeared,
5   Not by works of righteousness which we have done,
but according to his mercy he saved us, by the washing of
regeneration, and renewing of the Holy Ghost;

6   Which he shed on us abundantly through Jesus Christ our Saviour;
7   That being justified by his grace, we should be made heirs according to the hope of eternal life.

Before we can receive God's grace, we must acknowledge that we have sinned, realize that Jesus made the payment for our sins by shedding His blood on the Cross, and through faith accept that payment to receive eternal life. We can do nothing to earn God's favor; we must simply believe His promise and receive His grace. Faith is the trigger that releases grace to our lives.

Faith is not just an intellectual knowledge of the events of Christ's life; it is a transaction. Jesus called it being "born again." When we step beyond the knowing to the accepting of His sacrifice, we exchange our sin for Christ's righteousness. Grace is God's part; faith is our part. We exercise faith when we believe what the Bible says about God's plan, our sin, and His salvation.

B. By faith in Christ's work alone

Receiving God's grace only happens when we simply trust His work instead of our works. If you trust in your own abilities, you have no faith in Christ's work, and you will not receive grace. So many people try to earn what God offers freely. The hope that you can earn your way to Heaven insults Christ's sacrifice and denies the gift of salvation. What you are saying with this mindset is that Jesus' sacrifice is not enough for your salvation. Grace will never come to a heart that has not fully settled faith on Him and nothing else.

ROMANS 11:6

6   *And if by grace, then is it no more of works: otherwise grace is no more grace. But if it be of works, then is it no more grace: otherwise work is no more work.*

There is no middle ground between grace and works. You are either relying on grace completely or not at all. You are either claiming salvation because of God's gracious gift of His Son or because you believe you have earned it through your works. If you do not have Him only, you do not have Him at all.

Illustration

On a Marine Corps officer's sword you will find the slogan: "earned, never given." Grace is just the opposite: "given, never earned." Nothing we do earns us grace; Jesus Himself has completed the necessary work to provide the free gift of eternal life for us.

Conclusion

Because God has such a heart of love for us, He has provided through grace a plan both for our eternal life and for our temporal lives. Only through faith in Jesus' sacrifice for our sins is His grace applied to our lives. After salvation, grace transforms us from what we were into what God intends us to be.

Though grace is free to us, a very high price was paid— the precious blood of Jesus. Grace has great power—it redeems us, reclaims us, and renews us. We partake of God's grace through our faith in Christ's finished work on the Cross and that work alone—nothing more, nothing less.

During the Reformation, Martin Luther adopted a motto to summarize his teaching: "Grace alone, faith alone, Scripture alone." Anything we add to or take away from those essentials destroys their power. Trust in His grace—it is everything you will ever need.

Study Questions

1. How was the payment for grace made on our behalf?
   Sacrifice of Christ's love, sacrifice of Christ's blood

2. How did you first learn about God's grace?
   Answers will vary.

3. How is the power of grace demonstrated?
   Redeems us, reclaims us, renews us

4. What does it mean to be redeemed?
   To be released following the payment of a ransom

5. What lessons have you learned from grace in your life?
   Answers will vary.

6. How do we partake of the grace of God?
   Faith in Christ's work, faith in Christ's work alone

7. Why do people try to add things to grace rather than accept it?
   Answers will vary.

8. How can you most effectively share God's grace with others?
   Answers will vary.

Memory Verses

TITUS 2:11–13

11   For the grace of God that bringeth salvation hath appeared to all men,

12   Teaching us that, denying ungodliness and worldly lusts, we should live soberly, righteously, and godly, in this present world;

13   Looking for that blessed hope, and the glorious appearing of the great God and our Saviour Jesus Christ;

A Relieving Grace

Text

1 Kings 17:8–24

8   And the word of the Lord came unto him, saying,

9   Arise, get thee to Zarephath, which belongeth to Zidon, and dwell there: behold, I have commanded a widow woman there to sustain thee.

10   So he arose and went to Zarephath. And when he came to the gate of the city, behold, the widow woman was there gathering of sticks: and he called to her, and said, Fetch me, I pray thee, a little water in a vessel, that I may drink.

11   And as she was going to fetch it, he called to her, and said, Bring me, I pray thee, a morsel of bread in thine hand.

12   And she said, As the Lord thy God liveth, I have not a cake, but an handful of meal in a barrel, and a little oil in a cruse: and, behold, I am gathering two sticks, that I may go in and dress it for me and my son, that we may eat it, and die.

13   And Elijah said unto her, Fear not; go and do as thou hast said: but make me thereof a little cake first, and bring it unto me, and after make for thee and for thy son.

14   For thus saith the Lord God of Israel, The barrel of meal shall not waste, neither shall the cruse of oil fail, until the day that the Lord sendeth rain upon the earth.

15   And she went and did according to the saying of Elijah: and she, and he, and her house, did eat many days.

16   And the barrel of meal wasted not, neither did the cruse of oil fail, according to the word of the Lord, which he spake by Elijah.

91

17 And it came to pass after these things, that the son of the woman, the mistress of the house, fell sick; and his sickness was so sore, that there was no breath left in him.

18 And she said unto Elijah, What have I to do with thee, O thou man of God? art thou come unto me to call my sin to remembrance, and to slay my son?

19 And he said unto her, Give me thy son. And he took him out of her bosom, and carried him up into a loft, where he abode, and laid him upon his own bed.

20 And he cried unto the LORD, and said, O LORD my God, hast thou also brought evil upon the widow with whom I sojourn, by slaying her son?

21 And he stretched himself upon the child three times, and cried unto the LORD, and said, O LORD my God, I pray thee, let this child's soul come into him again.

22 And the LORD heard the voice of Elijah; and the soul of the child came into him again, and he revived.

23 And Elijah took the child, and brought him down out of the chamber into the house, and delivered him unto his mother: and Elijah said, See, thy son liveth.

24 And the woman said to Elijah, Now by this I know that thou art a man of God, and that the word of the LORD in thy mouth is truth.

Overview

Sometimes we think of grace only as a New Testament concept, but it is often seen in the Old Testament as well. In this Old Testament story, God demonstrates His grace in the life of the prophet Elijah. We see God's grace displayed in His provision not only for His prophet but also for the widow and her son.

We can be tempted to limit our thinking about grace to "church" matters, but it is for every need in life—physical, emotional, and spiritual. The relief that grace brings from the burdens and pressures we face cannot be found anywhere else: we must go to God to receive His grace during times of need.

Lesson Aim

We want the student to see how grace impacts our relationships with God and others and to understand how grace relieves the pressures we face and benefits our daily lives.

Lesson Goals

At the conclusion of the lesson, each student should:

1. Understand how grace helps him bear his burdens.
2. See the link between loving others and serving others.
3. Appreciate the Bible pattern of putting others first.
4. Rely on God's grace to meet physical and spiritual needs.
5. Know that grace can overcome even impossible obstacles.

Teaching Outline

  I. The Burden of the Widow
    A. Loneliness
    B. Limited resources
    C. Love

  II. The Belief of the Widow
    A. Faith to obey
    B. Grace to serve
      1. Grace to serve Elijah
      2. Grace to give to Elijah

III. The Blessings of the Widow
   A. Grace replenished her physical need.
   B. Grace relieved her fear.
      1. A tragic loss
      2. A tender prayer
      3. A triumphant resurrection

A Relieving Grace

Text

1 Kings 17:8–24

8   And the word of the Lord came unto him, saying,

9   Arise, get thee to Zarephath, which belongeth to Zidon, and dwell there: behold, I have commanded a widow woman there to sustain thee.

10   So he arose and went to Zarephath. And when he came to the gate of the city, behold, the widow woman was there gathering of sticks: and he called to her, and said, Fetch me, I pray thee, a little water in a vessel, that I may drink.

11   And as she was going to fetch it, he called to her, and said, Bring me, I pray thee, a morsel of bread in thine hand.

12   And she said, As the Lord thy God liveth, I have not a cake, but an handful of meal in a barrel, and a little oil in a cruse: and, behold, I am gathering two sticks, that I may go in and dress it for me and my son, that we may eat it, and die.

13 And Elijah said unto her, Fear not; go and do as thou hast said: but make me thereof a little cake first, and bring it unto me, and after make for thee and for thy son.

14 For thus saith the LORD God of Israel, The barrel of meal shall not waste, neither shall the cruse of oil fail, until the day that the LORD sendeth rain upon the earth.

15 And she went and did according to the saying of Elijah: and she, and he, and her house, did eat many days.

16 And the barrel of meal wasted not, neither did the cruse of oil fail, according to the word of the LORD, which he spake by Elijah.

17 And it came to pass after these things, that the son of the woman, the mistress of the house, fell sick; and his sickness was so sore, that there was no breath left in him.

18 And she said unto Elijah, What have I to do with thee, O thou man of God? art thou come unto me to call my sin to remembrance, and to slay my son?

19 And he said unto her, Give me thy son. And he took him out of her bosom, and carried him up into a loft, where he abode, and laid him upon his own bed.

20 And he cried unto the LORD, and said, O LORD my God, hast thou also brought evil upon the widow with whom I sojourn, by slaying her son?

21 And he stretched himself upon the child three times, and cried unto the LORD, and said, O LORD my God, I pray thee, let this child's soul come into him again.

22 And the LORD heard the voice of Elijah; and the soul of the child came into him again, and he revived.

23 And Elijah took the child, and brought him down out of the chamber into the house, and delivered him unto his mother: and Elijah said, See, thy son liveth.

24 And the woman said to Elijah, Now by this I know that thou art a man of God, and that the word of the LORD in thy mouth is truth.

Introduction

God always works graciously with people who trust and obey Him. Grace is not just for Bible characters or for others around you. If you are God's child, grace is for you. The story in 1 Kings 17 is a story of God's judging His people for turning away from Him. This passage may seem like a strange place to find grace, but even in His portrayal of judgment, God paints a picture of His grace, a reminder of His care and provision.

Because the people of Israel had turned to Baal, God, by His prophet Elijah, proclaimed a drought. This was a fitting judgment, for the people considered Baal to be a nature god in charge of the weather.

God promised to take care of Elijah during the drought. First God sent Elijah to a brook called Cherith, where he could drink from the stream and where He nourished him with food brought by ravens. When the brook dried up, God told Elijah to go to Zarephath. There a widow would care for him.

Obeying this commandment took faith on Elijah's part, because Zarephath belonged to Zidon—Jezebel's home country. Elijah was heading to the territory of the person who most wanted him dead. But he obeyed the Lord, and God showed him grace.

This story is not only about God's grace to Elijah, but it is also about how God used Elijah to be an instrument of His grace in the widow's life. We'll look first at the widow's burden, then at her faith, and finally at the blessings God showered on her by grace.

I.   The Burden of the Widow

1 Kings 17:9–12

9   Arise, get thee to Zarephath, which belongeth to Zidon, and dwell there: behold, I have commanded a widow woman there to sustain thee.

10 So he arose and went to Zarephath. And when he came to the gate of the city, behold, the widow woman was there gathering of sticks: and he called to her, and said, Fetch me, I pray thee, a little water in a vessel, that I may drink.
11 And as she was going to fetch it, he called to her, and said, Bring me, I pray thee, a morsel of bread in thine hand.
12 And she said, As the LORD thy God liveth, I have not a cake, but an handful of meal in a barrel, and a little oil in a cruse: and, behold, I am gathering two sticks, that I may go in and dress it for me and my son, that we may eat it, and die.

In Bible times, it was very difficult for a widow to provide for her children. That problem was compounded by a drought lasting years. In fact, the Bible tells us she was down to her last meal when Elijah came to her house. Anyone who has ever built a fire knows that if you have only two sticks, you are not planning on a big fire. She was preparing to die. But God had other plans—plans to manifest His amazing grace. Just as He has grace to relieve every burden she faced, He has grace to relieve every burden we face. He cares about your needs.

PSALM 146:9
9 The LORD preserveth the strangers; he relieveth the fatherless and widow: but the way of the wicked he turneth upside down.

A. Loneliness

We don't know how long it had been since the widow's husband had died, but now she had only her son to care for. She no longer had the companionship and comfort her husband had provided. She was all alone. She had to struggle to survive, shouldering the responsibilities that had been her husband's. The word *Zarephath* means "a melting place." For the widow, it was a place where her heart indeed had melted. She had suffered the loss of her husband, and when Elijah arrived, she was preparing for more devastation. She was desperately in need of God's grace and provision.

B. Limited resources

The drought had used up all that the widow had. She had only enough food left for one more meal and no possibility of more. Despite her own deprivation, despite her despair, we see that her concern was for her son. She was preparing to feed him one last time before they both died.

Illustration

A teacher asked a boy in her math class this question: "Suppose your mother baked a pie and there were seven of you—your parents and five children. What part of the pie would you get?" "One sixth," replied the boy.

"I'm afraid you don't know your fractions," said the teacher. "Remember, there are seven of you in your family."

"Yes, teacher," said the boy, "but you don't know my mother. Mother would say she didn't want any pie and cut it in six pieces."

JOB 36:15

15 *He delivereth the poor in his affliction, and openeth their ears in oppression.*

When we go through periods of scarcity, our temptation is to doubt God's love and goodness. We may feel that if He truly was gracious, we would have plenty.

That is certainly the message many churches teach today. We do not measure God's love by our material possessions; we measure His love by the grace He displayed on the Cross. The Cross is the substantiation that God will never fail to provide everything He deems necessary.

C. Love

We don't normally think of love as a burden, but it's impossible to truly love someone without being burdened for them. Everyone with a lost family member or a child who is away from God knows this burden well. The widow's love for her son was a constant burden as she struggled to keep him alive. Love meant that she cared about someone else more than she cared about herself, and her love was a burden she could never put down.

> **TEACHING TIP**
>
> *This is a great place to focus your class on the need for soulwinning in their own families. Allow some time for them to talk about unsaved loved ones. Relate that it is often harder to share the Gospel with those we know well than with strangers, and share your own stories of loved ones with whom you have shared Christ. Ask those with unsaved loved ones to make the commitment to witness to them during the next week. If the person lives too far away for a personal visit, encourage them to call or write.*

II. The Belief of the Widow

1 KINGS 17:15

15 *And she went and did according to the saying of Elijah: and she, and he, and her house, did eat many days.*

This widow was a woman of great faith. Though she did not have the Scriptures or the fellowship of other believers, she was open to following God's direction. From a human standpoint, Elijah's demand was outrageous. To ask a grieving mother to take food from the mouth of her starving child and give it to him instead was shocking. Yet, though his request went against all human reasoning, she did what the man of God told her to do.

She accepted the fact that she had a role to play in God's plan. People sometimes think that, because they have very little, they cannot or should not be involved in giving. But as we see from this widow's example, even when we suffer severe lack, we must still obey when God directs us to make sacrifices. Let's look at how she acted on her faith.

A. Faith to obey

When Elijah asked for a drink, the widow brought it to him. We don't know if her water was in as short supply as her food, but it is doubtful that she had much. When Elijah asked her to make his food before she made the last meal for herself and her son, she obeyed his instruction because of her faith.

Her response was quite different from that of Martha who objected when Jesus instructed the stone to be rolled away from the door of Lazarus' grave. She reasoned that after four days, the body would have begun to decompose. Relying on her own reasoning, she lacked faith. Look at Jesus' reply.

JOHN 11:40

40 Jesus saith unto her, Said I not unto thee, that, if thou wouldest believe, thou shouldest see the glory of God?

We see the demonstration of God's power only when we obey in faith. The challenge to Martha and the challenge to the widow were the same—to accept that what was impossible, humanly speaking, was possible with God and to obey without demanding to see an outcome first. God allowed the widow to exhaust her own resources before He intervened so that she could express her faith in Him through her actions. Had she received a miracle of provision first, no faith would have been required.

B. Grace to serve

The widow's response to Elijah shows grace in action as clearly as any other story in the Bible. Think about the ways she could have responded. If she had laughed and said, "You've got to be kidding," no one would have blamed her. Yet she *"went and did according to the saying of Elijah."* There is no record of questions, objections, or excuses, only of her obedience.

1. GRACE TO SERVE ELIJAH
PROVERBS 3:9–10
9 Honour the LORD with thy substance, and with the firstfruits of all thine increase:
10 So shall thy barns be filled with plenty, and thy presses shall burst out with new wine.

Putting God first takes grace because it goes against our nature. I believe the reason God sent Elijah to make that request of the widow was to demonstrate the importance of priorities. We must set aside our own interests and put Him first. Whether your substance is large or small, honor God with it first. Before God will pour out a blessing on anyone, He must be first in that individual's life (Matthew 6:33).

Someone said, "The way to tell whether you are a servant is how you act when you are treated like one." Are we putting others first? Do we serve others before we serve ourselves? Do we allow the grace of God to change our focus from what we can get and what we can enjoy to what we can give and how we can serve?

2. GRACE TO GIVE TO ELIJAH

MARK 12:41–44

41 And Jesus sat over against the treasury, and beheld how the people cast money into the treasury: and many that were rich cast in much.

42 And there came a certain poor widow, and she threw in two mites, which make a farthing.

43 And he called unto him his disciples, and saith unto them, Verily I say unto you, That this poor widow hath cast more in, than all they which have cast into the treasury:

44 For all they did cast in of their abundance; but she of her want did cast in all that she had, even all her living.

The story of Jesus' watching the widow giving her two mites at the temple is a perfect parallel to the story of the widow who fed Elijah. God watches when you are growing in grace, and He keeps record of your faithfulness. Whether we have much or little, grace equips us to give with a generous spirit and prepares our hearts to respond with a yes when we are asked to help.

Illustration

There is an old story about a man trying to cross a river. He didn't have money for the ferry ride, and the river was too deep to walk across. So the man stood by the road, watching men cross the river on horseback. After several men passed, he motioned to one and asked if he would be willing to carry him across. The man agreed and invited the waiting man to join him on his horse. When they reached the other side, he got off, thanked the rider, and watched him travel on. A man who had observed the crossing asked, "Why did you let those other men pass by and then ask General Andrew Jackson for a ride?" "I didn't know who he was," the man replied, "I was just looking for someone whose face said yes." Are other people willing to ask you for help? Does your face say yes to people in need?

2 CORINTHIANS 9:6–8
6   *But this I say, He which soweth sparingly shall reap also sparingly; and he which soweth bountifully shall reap also bountifully.*
7   *Every man according as he purposeth in his heart, so let him give; not grudgingly, or of necessity: for God loveth a cheerful giver.*
8   *And God is able to make all grace abound toward you; that ye, always having all sufficiency in all things, may abound to every good work:*

God is pleased with people who are willing givers. Jesus said the widow who gave two mites had given more than anyone else, not because of the amount of her gift, but because of the sacrifice and the spirit with which it was made.

Can you give sacrificially? When grace abounds in your life you can. Can you serve others? When grace abounds in your life you can. God never commands you to do anything He does not enable you to do. Instead of sitting back and waiting for the Christian life to make

sense to you, begin living in faith according to the Word
of God.

III. The Blessings of the Widow

1 KINGS 17:16

*16 And the barrel of meal wasted not, neither did the cruse
of oil fail, according to the word of the LORD, which he spake
by Elijah.*

When a person begins to grow in grace and exercise faith,
he can prepare for God to bless him and meet his needs. We
obey first, and then we are blessed. The widow trusted God
to keep His promise, and then He provided miraculously. As
Proverbs 3:34 says, *"he giveth grace unto the lowly."* The world
would not have ranked the widow as an important person,
but her humility and faith brought her a level of God's
blessing beyond that which most people ever experience.

A. *Grace replenished her physical need.*

The tiny amount of meal and oil that the widow had, a
portion only sufficient for one final meal, fed not only
two, but three people for "many days." God's grace is
sufficient. It is greater than your need, no matter what
your need is. Yet many children of God live without
experiencing the joy of seeing grace meet their needs.
Why not? God gives us the answer.

MATTHEW 9:28–29

*28 And when he was come into the house, the blind men
came to him: and Jesus saith unto them, Believe ye that I
am able to do this? They said unto him, Yea, Lord.*

29 *Then touched he their eyes, saying, According to your faith be it unto you.*

Is there anyone God cannot help? Is there a problem bigger than that which He can overcome? Do you face a challenging need that He cannot supply? Of course not. The problem is not His ability to provide, it is our reluctance to believe. Faith is required for grace to supply our needs.

B. Grace relieved her fear.

The great hymn "Amazing Grace" says:

> 'Twas grace that taught my heart to fear,
> And grace my fears relieved.

Grace can relieve our fears, yet fear remains a constant reality in America today. Mood-altering and anti-depressant drugs are some of the most commonly prescribed medications in our country.

The Bible tells us that a spirit of fear does not come from God (2 Timothy 1:7). We see this grace in the widow's life. Often after great victory, comes a great trial. After God miraculously provided her family's need, she lost the one thing in the world that she loved the most—her son.

1. A TRAGIC LOSS

1 KINGS 17:17–18

17 *And it came to pass after these things, that the son of the woman, the mistress of the house, fell sick; and his sickness was so sore, that there was no breath left in him.*

18 *And she said unto Elijah, What have I to do with thee, O thou man of God? art thou come unto me to call my sin to remembrance, and to slay my son?*

The only comfort that the widow had during the years without her husband was her son. He was her hope for the future. He was the one to whom she had dedicated her life. Now suddenly he was gone. Whatever hope and faith she had developed during those days of watching her meal and oil replenish disappeared in that moment of anguish.

Notice that she blamed Elijah for the death of her son. Had it not been for Elijah, her son would have starved to death long before. But many people respond to trouble irrationally, blaming God or supposing that God is judging their sins. In her grief, the widow responded both ways. While it is true that God chastens His children, not all trouble is a punishment for sin. We live in a fallen world, and trouble is a natural and normal part of life.

2.   A TENDER PRAYER

1 KINGS 17:19–21

19   *And he said unto her, Give me thy son. And he took him out of her bosom, and carried him up into a loft, where he abode, and laid him upon his own bed.*

20   *And he cried unto the LORD, and said, O LORD my God, hast thou also brought evil upon the widow with whom I sojourn, by slaying her son?*

21   *And he stretched himself upon the child three times, and cried unto the LORD, and said, O LORD my God, I pray thee, let this child's soul come into him again.*

Elijah's prayer for the boy is a great testimony to his faith. There is no record in Scripture of a resurrection prior to this story. He did not have previous examples to bolster his belief that God could resurrect the dead. But he had faith. Elijah believed that God was able to do whatever was needed to meet the need. Elijah believed that God would answer his prayer.

MATTHEW 21:22
22 And all things, whatsoever ye shall ask in prayer, believing, ye shall receive.

When we pray in faith, we can have confidence that God will answer. God's power is not confined to the past; it is real today. The question is whether we truly believe that He will answer our prayers. Many people say the words, but they have no confidence that their prayers will be answered. James said of a double-minded man—he who is not settled in his faith but wavers—*"let not that man think that he shall receive any thing of the Lord"* (James 1:7).

3. A TRIUMPHANT RESURRECTION
1 KINGS 17:22–24
22 And the LORD heard the voice of Elijah; and the soul of the child came into him again, and he revived.
23 And Elijah took the child, and brought him down out of the chamber into the house, and delivered him unto his mother: and Elijah said, See, thy son liveth.
24 And the woman said to Elijah, Now by this I know that thou art a man of God, and that the word of the LORD in thy mouth is truth.

Even if you are walking in the valley of the shadow of death, there is hope in the grace of God. Maybe it looks as if there is no hope for restoring your marriage. Maybe a child is breaking your heart, and you do not see how things will ever change. Maybe you have been passed over at work and fear that you will be stuck for the rest of your career. Nothing is impossible with God. You will never see more of God's grace than you will during the difficult and lonely times of your life.

If you had asked the widow to reveal her greatest fear, she almost certainly would have answered that something would happen to her son. When her greatest fear became reality, God bestowed abundant grace. We do not have to talk God into giving us grace; He gives us grace because He loves us so much. And through His grace, He meets and supplies our needs, blessing us in ways beyond what we can even imagine.

Conclusion

The testimony of this widow has endured for centuries. Jesus said, *"...many widows were in Israel...But unto none of them was Elias sent, save unto Sarepta, a city of Sidon, unto a woman that was a widow"* (Luke 4:25–26). Her life stands as a reminder of the importance of faith and the incredible power of grace to relieve the fears in our lives.

Grace takes our burdens and replaces them with God's blessings. Grace takes our fears and replaces them with God's peace. Grace provides the means for us to receive what we need from the Lord. Stop relying on your own strength, and allow God's grace to be made perfect in your weakness. You are not alone. God will never leave you nor forsake you (Hebrews 13:5). Let's return to "Amazing Grace" one more time:

> 'Tis grace that brought me safe thus far
> And grace will lead me home.

Study Questions

1. What burdens was the widow in 1 Kings 17 carrying?
   Loneliness, limited resources, love

2. What burdens are you carrying today?
   Answers will vary.

3. What burdens has grace helped you carry in the past?
   Answers will vary.

4. How was the widow's faith demonstrated?
   She obeyed Elijah's instructions.

5. In what way did grace help the widow serve Elijah?
   Served Elijah first; gave to Elijah

6. How did God's grace bless the widow?
   Replenished her physical need; relieved her fear

7. How did the widow respond to the death of her son?
   Blamed Elijah; thought she was being judged

8. How has grace relieved a fear in your life?
   Answers will vary.

Memory Verses

2 CORINTHIANS 9:6–8

6   But this I say, He which soweth sparingly shall reap also sparingly; and he which soweth bountifully shall reap also bountifully.

7   Every man according as he purposeth in his heart, so let him give; not grudgingly, or of necessity: for God loveth a cheerful giver.

8   And God is able to make all grace abound toward you; that ye, always having all sufficiency in all things, may abound to every good work:

A Rejoicing Grace

Text

COLOSSIANS 1:1–8

1 *Paul, an apostle of Jesus Christ by the will of God, and Timotheus our brother,*

2 *To the saints and faithful brethren in Christ which are at Colosse: Grace be unto you, and peace, from God our Father and the Lord Jesus Christ.*

3 *We give thanks to God and the Father of our Lord Jesus Christ, praying always for you,*

4 *Since we heard of your faith in Christ Jesus, and of the love which ye have to all the saints,*

5 *For the hope which is laid up for you in heaven, whereof ye heard before in the word of the truth of the gospel;*

6 *Which is come unto you, as it is in all the world; and bringeth forth fruit, as it doth also in you, since the day ye heard of it, and knew the grace of God in truth:*

7 *As ye also learned of Epaphras our dear fellowservant, who is for you a faithful minister of Christ;*

8 *Who also declared unto us your love in the Spirit.*

Overview

Grace changes everything. When God bestows grace on us, it transforms not only our eternal destiny but also the way we live and interact with others. As we look at Paul's letter to the church at Colosse, we can draw lessons about grace for our daily lives.

We'll look specifically at God's saving grace—what it is and then what it does.

Lesson Aim

We want the students to understand how grace impacts our words and how they can minister grace through their words, not only to the lost outside the church but also to struggling church members.

Lesson Goals

At the conclusion of the lesson, each student should:

1. Understand the way grace brings us salvation.
2. See the difference between grace and other "plans" of salvation.
3. Know the function of singing as an expression of grace.
4. Grasp the importance of using grace-filled words.
5. Take seriously his responsibility to be an encouragement to other believers.

Teaching Outline

I. The Presence of Saving Grace
   A. Commences at faith in Christ
   B. Continues throughout eternity
      1. In a heavenly home
      2. For all who believe

II. The Power of Singing Grace
   A. Because of a heart of peace
   B. Because of a heart of gratitude
   C. Because of a heart filled with God's Word

III. The Purpose of Speaking Grace
    A. Grace to speak the Gospel
        1. God prepared the way.
        2. Paul preached the Word.
    B. Grace to encourage others

A Rejoicing Grace

Text

COLOSSIANS 1:1–8

1 Paul, an apostle of Jesus Christ by the will of God, and Timotheus our brother,

2 To the saints and faithful brethren in Christ which are at Colosse: Grace be unto you, and peace, from God our Father and the Lord Jesus Christ.

3 We give thanks to God and the Father of our Lord Jesus Christ, praying always for you,

4 Since we heard of your faith in Christ Jesus, and of the love which ye have to all the saints,

5 For the hope which is laid up for you in heaven, whereof ye heard before in the word of the truth of the gospel;

6 Which is come unto you, as it is in all the world; and bringeth forth fruit, as it doth also in you, since the day ye heard of it, and knew the grace of God in truth:

7   As ye also learned of Epaphras our dear fellowservant, who is for you a faithful minister of Christ;

8   Who also declared unto us your love in the Spirit.

Introduction

Paul's epistle to the church at Colosse is unusual in that it is written to a church he did not start. He had *"heard of* [their] *faith"* but did not win them personally. The pastor of the church at Colosse was Epaphras who, many scholars believe, was saved at Ephesus and traveled to Colosse where he started a church. Epaphras visited Paul while he was imprisoned in Rome, and during that visit, Paul wrote this letter for Epaphras to take back to his congregation.

Because of the prevalence of false teaching in their culture, Paul wanted to encourage these Christians to develop into mature believers. He began and ended his letter of encouragement with grace. To counter the influences of their culture, the church at Colosse needed God's grace just as we do today. Living apart from the power of grace results in negative feelings—disappointment, discouragement, and depression. Our lives do not have to be characterized by these things; we can live with peace and joy instead of living like the unsaved who do not know God's grace.

COLOSSIANS 2:8–9

8   Beware lest any man spoil you through philosophy and vain deceit, after the tradition of men, after the rudiments of the world, and not after Christ.

9   For in him dwelleth all the fulness of the Godhead bodily.

Many churches today are adopting the world's philosophies rather than remaining faithful to the doctrines of Jesus Christ. The result is they are being spoiled—not like rotten fruit, but in the way an invading army carries treasures away. Trusting human wisdom and understanding rather than God's Word spoils us of the riches and the rejoicing that come through grace. Let's look at the riches of grace Paul describes in the book of Colossians.

I. The Presence of Saving Grace

Saving grace is the most important aspect of God's grace. Notice that Paul starts his letter with *"grace and peace."* That is always God's order. Apart from grace, there is no peace with God. Because the Colossians had experienced saving grace, they had access to the power of God working in their lives. What does the Bible tell us about the presence of grace in our lives?

A. *Commences at faith in Christ*

EPHESIANS 2:8–9

8   *For by grace are ye saved through faith; and that not of yourselves: it is the gift of God:*

9   *Not of works, lest any man should boast.*

The only way to obtain grace is to receive it as a gift by faith in Jesus Christ. It is not earned or merited. Complete trust in Him is the only way to experience God's saving grace. Grace is God's part in salvation; faith is ours. Men are always seeking to earn salvation. But being baptized, doing good works, giving to the poor, living an upright life, and joining a church do not take us a single step closer to Heaven. We have nothing to boast of in regard to our salvation. We are not saved because of what we do; we are saved because of the sacrifice Jesus made on our behalf.

As a Roman Catholic monk, Martin Luther struggled with the weight of his sin. Unable to find relief through the Roman Catholic teachings or his own self-inflicted penance, Luther found the truth in God's Word. While meditating on the phrase, *"the just shall live by faith"* (Romans 1:17), he finally understood God's freely offered grace and put his faith in Christ alone for salvation. In that moment, the truth of grace began to spark the Reformation.

B. Continues throughout eternity

In verse 5 Paul talks about the hope laid up for us in Heaven. Paul is not referring to our hope of *going* to Heaven, which is a wonderful assurance. He is referring to the rejoicing we will experience when we enter into the presence of God. Those of us who are saved have so much waiting for us to enjoy. For all of eternity, we will continue to enjoy the riches of God's grace.

1.   IN A HEAVENLY HOME
JOHN 14:1–3

1   Let not your heart be troubled: ye believe in God, believe also in me.

2   In my Father's house are many mansions: if it were not so, I would have told you. I go to prepare a place for you.

3   And if I go and prepare a place for you, I will come again, and receive you unto myself; that where I am, there ye may be also.

Jesus made a promise: He will take us to a place He has prepared, and we will be with Him forever. He made a personal promise, and He will keep it. One day soon, we are going to see the beauty of Heaven because of His grace. In our eternal home, there will be no sorrow, no pain, and no death. This promise gives us comfort and hope no matter what circumstances we may face.

Illustration

I read a story about a grandmother who took her granddaughter out for a walk on a beautiful moonlit evening. The stars were magnificent that night. As they walked together, she named individual stars and constellations for the little girl. As they looked up at the sky, her granddaughter exclaimed, "Grandma, if the bottom side of Heaven is this beautiful, just think how wonderful the top side must be!"

2. FOR ALL WHO BELIEVE

2 THESSALONIANS 2:16

16 Now our Lord Jesus Christ himself, and God, even our Father, which hath loved us, and hath given us everlasting consolation and good hope through grace.

JOHN 1:17

17 For the law was given by Moses, but grace and truth came by Jesus Christ.

Everyone who has placed his faith in Jesus has the hope of this eternal home. Those who have gone before us in faith are already enjoying what has been prepared for us. Heaven is our hope for the future, and because it is the promise of God, it is sure, just as if we were already there.

With this hope buoying our spirits and the Holy Spirit bearing fruit in our lives, we can have grace to lift up His name in song, expressing our thanks and worship from hearts of love. As we acknowledge and live in the presence of saving grace, we gain access to the power of singing grace, and our worship brings honor and glory to Him.

II. The Power of Singing Grace

EPHESIANS 5:18–19

18 And be not drunk with wine, wherein is excess; but be filled with the Spirit;
19 Speaking to yourselves in psalms and hymns and spiritual songs, singing and making melody in your heart to the Lord;

God's people throughout history have been a singing people. It was true of the Old Testament Jews who used the book of Psalms as their hymnbook for worship. It was true of the New Testament church, and it is still true today. Martin Luther said, "Our dear fathers and prophets did not desire without reason that music be always used in the churches. Hence, we have so many songs and psalms. This precious gift has been given to man alone that he might thereby remind himself that God has created man for the express purpose of praising and extolling God."

A. Because of a heart of peace

COLOSSIANS 3:15–16

15 And let the peace of God rule in your hearts, to the which also ye are called in one body; and be ye thankful.
16 Let the word of Christ dwell in you richly in all wisdom; teaching and admonishing one another in psalms and hymns and spiritual songs, singing with grace in your hearts to the Lord.

The peace of God is a direct result of the grace of God. The order that we see in the Scriptures is first grace, then peace—always. The peace that comes from God's grace gives us reason to sing regardless of the circumstances. Paul and Silas, when they were incarcerated in Philippi, having been beaten and wrongfully imprisoned, were still able to sing because they had God's peace even during painful circumstances (Acts 16:25).

The songs, hymns, and spiritual songs mentioned in Ephesians 5 are all expressions of the gratitude and worship that exist in our hearts as we are filled with the Holy Spirit. The grace of God leads to thankful, singing believers. Just the joy of knowing we are saved by grace gives us reason to sing. He who has not obtained saving grace will not have the peace that produces a singing heart. Charles Spurgeon said, "Settle the center, and the circumference is secure."

B. Because of a heart of gratitude

Discouragement quiets our singing when we lose sight of the incredible work God has done for us. By maintaining a proper focus on the miracle of our salvation freely received through grace, we recognize hundreds of reasons to sing. Singing is the natural outgrowth of a thankful heart. That's why Colossians 3:15 instructs us to be thankful. Dr. Bob Jones Sr. said, "When gratitude dies on the altar of a man's heart, that man is well nigh hopeless."

2 CORINTHIANS 4:13–15

13 *We having the same spirit of faith, according as it is written, I believed, and therefore have I spoken; we also believe, and therefore speak;*

14 Knowing that he which raised up the Lord Jesus shall raise up us also by Jesus, and shall present us with you.
15 For all things are for your sakes, that the abundant grace might through the thanksgiving of many redound to the glory of God.

Singing and offering thanks as an expression of our gratitude brings glory to God. Instead of taking credit for the good things in our lives, we are giving the credit to the only One who deserves it. And singing in gratitude, even during difficult times, is a powerful testimony to those around us that the grace of God is real.

C. Because of a heart filled with God's Word

As the Word dwells in us richly, we will be singing Christians. In Colossians 3:16, the word *dwell* means "to be at home." We must memorize and meditate on the Word of God so that it is at home in our hearts. We also need to be part of a church that preaches and teaches the Scriptures, to help us grow in grace. Only the Bible has the power to transform our lives.

JOHN 5:39–40
39 Search the scriptures; for in them ye think ye have eternal life: and they are they which testify of me.
40 And ye will not come to me, that ye might have life.

Illustration

We have a father in our church who lost his wife when his children were still young. The testimony he showed to our church and our community was a testimony of grace. He said to me, "I'm just claiming Isaiah 50:7 and Romans 8:28." How was he able to walk through the valley of the shadow of death without despair? The Word of God was dwelling in his heart. I've seen people become bitter and fall apart in a trial like that, but he had God's peace and God's grace because God's Word had done a transforming work in his life.

TEACHING TIP

Involve your students in discovering specific Bible truths that will help them apply these lessons to their lives. For example, ask them to name truths about which they can sing and rejoice regardless of difficult circumstances. You may want to give them one or two examples from the list below to help them get started.

Truths to Keep You Singing!
- *God's love for me is unchanging. (Romans 8:31–32; Jeremiah 31:3; 1 John 4:10)*
- *God's purpose for me is Christ-likeness. (Romans 8:28–29; Colossians 1:28; Ephesians 4:11–13)*
- *God's Word has the right answers. (2 Timothy 3:15–16; Hebrews 4:12; 1 John 5:3; Deuteronomy 6:6–9)*
- *God's grace is sufficient. (2 Corinthians 12:9; 2 Timothy 2:1; Titus 2:11–12; Romans 5:20–21)*

III. The Purpose of Speaking Grace

COLOSSIANS 4:3–6

3 *Withal praying also for us, that God would open unto us a door of utterance, to speak the mystery of Christ, for which I am also in bonds:*

4   That I may make it manifest, as I ought to speak.
5   Walk in wisdom toward them that are without, redeeming the time.
6   Let your speech be alway with grace, seasoned with salt, that ye may know how ye ought to answer every man.

Though Paul was in prison when he wrote this epistle, he did not ask the church at Colosse to pray for his release from captivity. Instead, he asked them to pray for his effectiveness as he worked to win souls, even in prison. A man who requests prayer for soulwinning instead of deliverance is a man who has grown in the grace of the Lord Jesus Christ. Let's look at the two specific kinds of speaking grace that we find in Scripture.

A. Grace to speak the Gospel

Every person who shares the Gospel needs the grace of God. We cannot win souls in our own strength and power; the Holy Spirit must do *His* work of grace through us.

In verse 3, Paul talked about speaking *"the mystery of Christ."* When we think of a mystery, we usually think about a detective trying to solve a case. But in Scripture, a mystery is something hidden that needs to be revealed. In his letter to Timothy, Paul used the word *mystery* in this sense.

1 TIMOTHY 3:16
16   And without controversy great is the mystery of godliness: God was manifest in the flesh, justified in the Spirit, seen of angels, preached unto the Gentiles, believed on in the world, received up into glory.

1. GOD PREPARED THE WAY.

In response to these prayers, God gave Paul opportunities to present the Gospel to individuals for whom the Gospel had previously been a mystery. In jail, in Jewish synagogues, and in the meeting places of Greek cities, Paul revealed the wonderful mystery of God's grace.

2. PAUL PREACHED THE WORD.

EPHESIANS 6:19–20

19 *And for me, that utterance may be given unto me, that I may open my mouth boldly, to make known the mystery of the gospel,*

20 *For which I am an ambassador in bonds: that therein I may speak boldly, as I ought to speak.*

Many churches in America have changed their message. They talk about current events. They tell interesting, amusing, or heart-warming stories. But because they do not preach the Word of God, few souls are saved, and few lives are transformed. Never forget that the Bible is God's only message to share with a lost and dying world.

B. Grace to encourage others

Sharing the Gospel is not the only reason to speak with grace; the Bible commands us to have gracious speech that is "seasoned with salt" to be an encouragement to others. We live in a world of discouragement. It seems that someone is always ready to inform you how much you fall short or why your plans will fail. Discouragers are more than happy to describe in great detail the insurmountable obstacles you will face. With all of these negative messages bombarding us, we need to hear encouraging words, and others need encouragement from us.

I heard of a man who opened his front door to get the morning newspaper and was surprised to see a little dog sitting there with the paper in his mouth. Delighted with this unexpected "delivery service," he fed the dog some treats. The following morning he was unpleasantly surprised to see the same dog sitting in front of his door, wagging his tail, surrounded by eight newspapers! When you give encouragement you get results!

EPHESIANS 4:29
29 Let no corrupt communication proceed out of your mouth, but that which is good to the use of edifying, that it may minister grace unto the hearers.

If your speech is filled with bitterness and anger, your words will dishearten those who hear them. But if your words are filled with grace, you will build up those who listen. Every Christian is called to a full-time ministry. You may not be a pastor or a teacher, but as you travel the path God has laid for you, you are to be a minister of God's grace through your uplifting words. Warren Wiersbe said, "With grace on our hearts and lips, we will be faithful witnesses and not judges and prosecuting attorneys."

Conclusion

The grace of God is an integral part of every aspect of the Christian life. Having saving grace gives us the peace and joy to have singing grace. Are you able to keep a song in your heart no matter what happens around you? If not, you need to experience this work of grace in your life. Finally, we need God's grace for sharing the Gospel with others and for encouraging believers within the church. Your words are a powerful witness to the presence, or possibly the absence, of grace in your heart.

Study Questions

1. How do we receive God's saving grace?
    Through faith in Jesus Christ

2. How and when did you receive God's saving grace?
    Answers will vary.

3. What three kinds of music does the Bible talk about?
    Psalms, hymns, spiritual songs

4. What three things in our heart will make us singing Christians?
    A heart of peace, a heart of gratitude, a heart filled with God's Word

5. What has God done for you that you would like to share with the class?
    Answers will vary.

6. In what two specific areas of speech do we need God's grace?
    To preach the Gospel; to encourage others

7. What does the Bible mean when it talks about a "mystery"?
    Something that is hidden that is to be revealed

8. Who have you shared the Gospel with recently and what was the result?
    Answers will vary.

Memory Verses

EPHESIANS 5:18–19

18   *And be not drunk with wine, wherein is excess; but be filled with the Spirit;*

19   *Speaking to yourselves in psalms and hymns and spiritual songs, singing and making melody in your heart to the Lord;*

A Restraining Grace

Text

TITUS 2:11–15

11 *For the grace of God that bringeth salvation hath appeared to all men,*

12 *Teaching us that, denying ungodliness and worldly lusts, we should live soberly, righteously, and godly, in this present world;*

13 *Looking for that blessed hope, and the glorious appearing of the great God and our Saviour Jesus Christ;*

14 *Who gave himself for us, that he might redeem us from all iniquity, and purify unto himself a peculiar people, zealous of good works.*

15 *These things speak, and exhort, and rebuke with all authority. Let no man despise thee.*

Overview

Grace is one of the most misunderstood and mischaracterized doctrines in the Word of God. Many people deliberately misconstrue grace to mean that, when a person possesses grace, he has the right to do anything he chooses. But God's Word does not give the Christian a license to live an unrestrained life.

Grace does offer us many gifts, most importantly, of course, is our salvation. But grace also places guidelines on our lives by teaching us to deny ungodliness and worldly lusts so that we can live sober, righteous, and godly lives. And the goodness of grace gives us a certain hope and expectation for the future.

Lesson Aim

We want the student to understand the true meaning of grace rather than accept the false pretense that grace gives them license to do whatever they want.

Lesson Goals

At the conclusion of the lesson, each student should:

1. Understand why God gives us His grace.
2. Recognize the purpose of our salvation.
3. Know the lessons that grace teaches about how we should live.
4. See the way grace leads toward godly living.
5. Have a renewed expectation of the Second Coming.

Teaching Outline

I. The Gift of Grace
   A. Grace brings salvation.
      1. Salvation is through Christ.
      2. Salvation accompanies redemption.
   B. Grace bought our salvation.
      1. It is for all men.
      2. It is free for all men.

II. The Guidance of Grace
   A. Guidance away from ungodliness
      1. Deny ungodliness.
      2. Deny worldly lusts.

   B.   Guidance toward a sanctified life
1. We should live soberly.
2. We should live righteously.
3. We should live godly.

III. The Goodness of Grace
   A.   We have an expectation of Christ.
1. It is an anticipated time.
2. It is a happy time.
   B.   We will see the exaltation of Christ.
1. A glorious appearing
2. A personal appearing

A Restraining Grace

Text

TITUS 2:11–15

11 *For the grace of God that bringeth salvation hath appeared to all men,*

12 *Teaching us that, denying ungodliness and worldly lusts, we should live soberly, righteously, and godly, in this present world;*

13 *Looking for that blessed hope, and the glorious appearing of the great God and our Saviour Jesus Christ;*

14 *Who gave himself for us, that he might redeem us from all iniquity, and purify unto himself a peculiar people, zealous of good works.*

15 *These things speak, and exhort, and rebuke with all authority. Let no man despise thee.*

Introduction

Titus is one of the pastoral epistles—letters that Paul wrote to Timothy and Titus—written to instruct pastors on the oversight of the church. Titus spent most of his ministry on the island of Crete, where the church had doctrinal issues. These led, as is always the case, to behavioral issues. When we do not believe right, we will not behave right.

Misinterpreting grace was one of their great doctrinal issues. Some people were taking advantage of the grace of God, teaching that, because they were forgiven, they could live however they wanted to live "under grace." One of the main purposes of the book of Titus was to straighten out this misunderstanding. It is true that we are no longer bound to the law, that we do not gain or keep our salvation by our works. Yet under grace, we have an even greater responsibility than did people who lived under the law.

Presuming on the grace of God by willfully doing wrong is one of the most dangerous things a believer can do. Grace does free us from the bondage of sin, but more than that, it prescribes for us a new lifestyle—one of restraint. To help us understand the true meaning and purpose of grace, we're going to look at the gift of grace, the guidance of grace, and the goodness of grace.

I. The Gift of Grace

We must never forget that grace is completely unmerited—a gift of God (Ephesians 2:8–9). The only way we can receive grace is to accept it as a free gift, just as God offers it to us. And with grace come numerous gifts that God bestows upon us.

A. Grace brings salvation.

The most important gift that we can ever receive is the gift of salvation, which comes through grace. Over and over again the Bible emphasizes that grace is our only hope of salvation. In the classic hymn "Rock of Ages," Augustus Toplady wrote:

> Not the labors of my hands
> Can fulfill Thy law's commands;
> Could my zeal no respite know,
> Could my tears forever flow
> All for sin could not atone;
> Thou must save, and Thou alone.

1. SALVATION IS THROUGH CHRIST.

1 PETER 2:24

24 Who his own self bare our sins in his own body on the tree, that we, being dead to sins, should live unto righteousness: by whose stripes ye were healed.

Jesus Christ came to this earth, born of the virgin Mary. He lived a perfectly sinless life, though He was tempted in all points just as we are (Hebrews 4:15). When His ministry was complete, He willingly laid down His life for us on the Cross, making the payment for all of our sins. He rose from the dead and returned to His Father in Heaven. No one else could have done what Jesus did. No one else was qualified to pay for the sins of the world. It was because of grace that Jesus paid the price for our salvation.

2. SALVATION ACCOMPANIES REDEMPTION.

ROMANS 3:24

24 Being justified freely by his grace through the redemption that is in Christ Jesus:

Since the Fall, man has been under sin. Sin separated us from God and brought us under Satan's control. Since each of us has sinned, we must each be redeemed—delivered or liberated by the payment God demands for our sin.

Illustration

One of the most famous court cases in our country's history was the Dred Scott decision in 1857. Scott was born a slave in Virginia around 1800. On the death of his original master, Peter Blow, he was sold to an army surgeon who was stationed in many states, including Illinois. When Dr. Emerson died, Scott sued for his freedom on the grounds that he had lived for a number of years in a state where slavery was illegal. After an eleven-year battle, the Supreme Court ruled that Scott had no rights of citizenship and would have to remain a slave. Having sympathy on his plight, the sons of Peter Blow, Scott's original owner, purchased him back and gave him his freedom as well as that of his wife and two daughters. (information taken from http://www.pbs.org/wgbh/aia/part4/4p2932.html)

B. Grace bought our salvation.

The only way we can have salvation is if the price for it is paid. That is what grace does—it provides complete payment for a debt that we could never pay on our own. Though salvation is free to us, Christ certainly paid a great price to purchase this gift. If we could do something to earn or deserve salvation, we would be making a payment, not receiving a gift. Grace has already paid the full price with the precious blood of Jesus Christ.

1.   It is for all men. (Titus 2:11)

John 3:15–16

15   That whosoever believeth in him should not perish, but have eternal life.

16   For God so loved the world, that he gave his only begotten Son, that whosoever believeth in him should not perish, but have everlasting life.

John 4:13–14

13   Jesus answered and said unto her, Whosoever drinketh of this water shall thirst again:

14   But whosoever drinketh of the water that I shall give him shall never thirst; but the water that I shall give him shall be in him a well of water springing up into everlasting life.

Some churches teach that grace is only available to a select group of people. I am thankful that God loves all of us. A song often taught in Sunday school is "Jesus Loves the Little Children." If grace is not for all men, then that song isn't true. But the Bible teaches over and over again the truth of "whosoever"—that salvation is available to everyone who believes. The offer of God's grace is not restricted.

2.   It is free for all men.

Romans 6:23

23   For the wages of sin is death; but the gift of God is eternal life through Jesus Christ our Lord.

Many religions teach doing good works, in addition to believing in Jesus, for salvation. If, at the end of our lives, salvation were contingent on our good outweighing our bad, none of us would ever see Heaven. If you have never experienced the free gift of grace, there is no better time than today for you to accept by faith the payment Jesus made to purchase your salvation.

II. The Guidance of Grace

God has designed the Christian life for growth in grace. Every Christian has received the gift of grace, but not every Christian grows in that grace. To experience growth, we must learn the same lessons about grace that Paul shared with Titus. The same grace that brought us salvation *teaches* ("to train as with children, causing them to learn; to chastise, or to correct") us how to live as God intends. Grace does not become dormant after salvation; it remains an active, vital, working part of our lives.

Salvation is the miracle of a moment, but growing in grace is the process of a lifetime. Warren Wiersbe said, "Grace not only redeems us, but it also reforms us and rewards us." Grace continues to develop our hearts as long as we yield to the leading of the Holy Spirit of God. Notice that grace guides us away from some things and toward some others.

A. Guidance away from ungodliness

A Christian who is growing in grace will be moving away from things that are displeasing to the Lord. God is not interested in withholding good things from us; after all, He did not withhold His Son. But He wants us to avoid things that destroy our souls and damage our testimonies. Years ago a preacher said, "If you give a pig and a boy everything they want, you'll get a good pig and a bad boy."

1. DENY UNGODLINESS.

To deny means "not to accept, to reject, to refuse something offered." God's grace teaches His children to refuse the lifestyle of the world. *Ungodliness* in this passage entails more than just irreverence; it means a total lack of recognition of God's presence. It is "to ignore His influence, existence or expectation." It is possible for a child of God to refuse the teaching of grace and live in ungodliness, but there are severe consequences to such behavior. The Holy Spirit gives us an early warning system to stay away from certain things, and we need to be attentive to those warnings.

Illustration

I went to the doctor for a checkup some time ago. He told me that his area of expertise was early detection. He said, "I try to see the symptoms of problems before they become major. The earlier we detect a problem, the better chance we have to fix it." As I thought about his words, I realized that God has placed the Holy Spirit in my life as an early detection system. Many times He has taught me to deny some things because He wants to guide me away from ungodliness.

2. DENY WORLDLY LUSTS.

GALATIANS 5:13

13 *For, brethren, ye have been called unto liberty; only use not liberty for an occasion to the flesh, but by love serve one another.*

ROMANS 5:20–6:2

20 *Moreover the law entered, that the offence might abound. But where sin abounded, grace did much more abound:*

21 That as sin hath reigned unto death, even so might grace reign through righteousness unto eternal life by Jesus Christ our Lord.
6:1 What shall we say then? Shall we continue in sin, that grace may abound?
2 God forbid. How shall we, that are dead to sin, live any longer therein?

Lust is a desire, a longing for the forbidden. Grace is not a license to fulfill these fleshly cravings, though many would have us to believe so with their erroneous teaching that grace covers all, allowing us to sin willfully without consequences. The Bible teaches just the opposite. Though He is gracious, He remains just and holy and will not overlook a violation of His commandments. We must not abuse the grace of God.

How we live does matter to God. He commands us to be dead to sin and alive to God. Christians who understand grace properly do not willfully live in sin; grace draws them away from sin and toward God.

B. Guidance toward a sanctified life

The battery in your car has both a positive and a negative terminal, and you need both, or the car won't run. Grace is the same way. It has both a negative pull, drawing us *away from* sin, and a positive pull, drawing us *toward* righteousness. Someone taught by the Holy Spirit will strive to live by these three positive principles.

1. WE SHOULD LIVE SOBERLY.

To *live soberly* means "to live with a sound mind, to demonstrate a temperate, self-controlled life." We cannot produce this demeanor through our own effort; rather, self-control is one characteristic of the Holy Spirit's fruit in our lives. When someone treats us wrongly, but we choose to forgive rather than retaliate, we are being guided by the Spirit through grace instead of responding in the flesh.

2.   WE SHOULD LIVE RIGHTEOUSLY.

To *live righteously* means "to live an upright and proper life." The problem of unrighteousness in our nation today is not that politicians are hostile to religion or that temptation lurks on every hand; the problem is that God's people are not willing to follow the teaching of grace and the guidance of the Holy Spirit to live according to God's direction.

3.   WE SHOULD LIVE GODLY.

1 THESSALONIANS 1:9

9   *For they themselves shew of us what manner of entering in we had unto you, and how ye turned to God from idols to serve the living and true God;*

To *live godly* means "living with a consciousness of God's presence." It is a realization that every moment of our lives His Spirit is with us, hearing every word, seeing every deed, pondering every thought. God wants our lives to be holy to such a degree that we stand out from the world and bring honor and glory to Him. Grace is meant to make a difference not only in our eternal destiny but also in our earthly lives. On this earthly journey we need to be guided by His grace.

Illustration

Elizabeth Elliot tells of two adventurers who visited her in the South American jungle. Loaded with equipment for a trek into the rain forest, they sought no advice before embarking; they just wanted to learn a few phrases to converse with the Indians they might meet. She wrote later: "Sometimes we come to God as the two adventurers came to me—confident and, we think, well-informed and well-equipped. But has it occurred to us that with all our accumulation of stuff, something is missing?"

She suggests that we often ask God for too little. We know what we need—a "yes" or "no" answer to our question or perhaps a road sign. Too often we look for something quick and easy to point us through this life, when what we really need is the Guide Himself. Maps, road signs, and a few useful phrases are important things, but infinitely better is Someone who has walked the road before us, who understands every temptation and difficulty and wants to help us overcome every obstacle we will face.

TEACHING TIP

Because what the Bible teaches about grace is so different from what many of the members of your class will have heard from preachers on television or in popular books, stop and reinforce the truths we have just seen regarding both the positive and negative aspects of grace. Ask the class members to discuss things that the Holy Spirit has led them to do or to avoid doing as part of their growth in grace. Try to balance the discussion so that the lessons of grace are neither all positive nor all negative.

III. The Goodness of Grace

It is grace that gives us hope for the future. We are not alone. God did not save us then abandon us to make it on our own. As one verse in "Amazing Grace" says:

> 'Tis grace that brought me safe thus far
> And grace will lead me home.

A. We have an expectation of Christ.

Paul told Titus that grace teaches us to look for the return of the Lord. In verse 13, *looking for* means "to receive one from somewhere else; to accept a thing offered; to expect the fulfillment of a promise." The return of Christ could happen at any moment. No further prophetic events must happen before He appears. He could come today, and we are to be looking forward to His return.

1. IT IS AN ANTICIPATED TIME.

We are not just to be waiting for His return; we are to be eager for it. Paul told Timothy that there is a reward, a crown of righteousness, for *"all them also that love his appearing"* (2 Timothy 4:8). Are you ready for Him to return, or do you need more time to set things in order so that you will not be ashamed at His coming?

Illustration

While on a South Pole expedition, British explorer Sir Ernest Shackleton found his ship, the *Endurance*, trapped in early ice and then crushed. The crew escaped to an ice floe and floated north until they were close enough to take the lifeboats they had salvaged to nearby Elephant Island. Shackleton ordered out one lifeboat modified for

147

the open sea, and left twenty-two men behind, promising them that he would return to rescue them. After more than two weeks at sea, which included surviving a major hurricane, Shackleton reached a whaling station where he found help.

When he tried to go back to rescue his crew, huge icebergs blocked the way. But on his fourth attempt, suddenly, as if by a miracle, an avenue opened in the ice, and Shackleton was able to get through. His men, ready and waiting, though more than four months had passed, quickly scrambled aboard. No sooner had the ship cleared the island than the ice crashed together behind them. Contemplating their narrow escape, the explorer said to his men, "It was fortunate you were all packed and ready to go!" They replied, "We never gave up hope. Whenever the sea was clear of ice, we rolled up our sleeping bags and reminded each other, 'The boss may come today.'"

2. IT IS A HAPPY TIME.

The Bible calls the return of Christ "the blessed hope." For those preparing to meet Him by living according to the teachings of grace, it will be a time of rejoicing and celebration. We have a joyful expectation that His promise will be fulfilled and that we will meet our Saviour.

1 THESSALONIANS 1:10

10 And to wait for his Son from heaven, whom he raised from the dead, even Jesus, which delivered us from the wrath to come.

1 JOHN 3:1–3

1 Behold, what manner of love the Father hath bestowed upon us, that we should be called the sons of God: therefore the world knoweth us not, because it knew him not.

2 Beloved, now are we the sons of God, and it doth not yet appear what we shall be: but we know that, when he shall appear, we shall be like him; for we shall see him as he is.

3 And every man that hath this hope in him purifieth himself, even as he is pure.

Notice that the hope of the Second Coming is a powerful motivator for us. We have no greater incentive for godly living than the fact that Jesus is coming again. When company is coming to your house, you make preparations. Everything is cleaned and straightened up so that you will not be embarrassed when your guests arrive. If you have things in your heart that need to be changed and you truly believe that the Lord's return is imminent, you will not delay in making the necessary changes.

Illustration

After church one Sunday, a little girl who had been taught about the Second Coming in her class was quizzing her mother.

"Mommy, do you believe Jesus will come back?"

"Yes."

"Could it be today?"

"Yes."

"Could it be in a few minutes?"

"Yes, dear."

"Mommy, would you comb my hair?"

B. We will see the exaltation of Christ.

When Jesus came to Earth the first time, He emptied Himself of the glory that was rightfully His as the Son of God. Except for a brief moment on the Mount of Transfiguration, He was never seen in the full brightness of His person. But when He returns, He is going to be clothed in honor and glory, and He will be highly exalted.

PHILIPPIANS 2:9–11

9 Wherefore God also hath highly exalted him, and given him a name which is above every name:
10 That at the name of Jesus every knee should bow, of things in heaven, and things in earth, and things under the earth;
11 And that every tongue should confess that Jesus Christ is Lord, to the glory of God the Father.

1. A GLORIOUS APPEARING

We will be witnesses to His exaltation as the King and Ruler of the Universe. The Greek word used here is *doxa*, from which we get the word *doxology*. It speaks of praise and glory directed at the very essence and person of Jesus, who is worthy of all honor. On that day, He will be crowned with the kingly majesty that belongs to Him as supreme Ruler—majesty in the sense of the absolute perfection of the Deity. The appearing of the Lord will be such an occasion as the world has never seen.

2. A PERSONAL APPEARING

The Second Coming is the return of our Lord and Saviour Jesus Christ. And our text leaves no doubt about the deity of Jesus Christ. He is directly called the "great

God," a clear statement indicating that He is far more than a good man or a wise teacher. False cults and false religions deny the deity of Jesus, but the Bible is quite clear that Jesus is God manifest in the flesh.

Conclusion

This passage in Titus walks us through the complete process of grace in the Christian life. We begin our walk with God when we are saved by grace through faith. Continuing our walk with God, we grow in grace as we yield to the direction of the Holy Spirit and learn the lessons grace teaches about how we should live. Finally, grace gives us hope for the future. No matter what comes into our lives, we have the certain promise that Jesus will return and claim us for His own.

A proper understanding of what grace really is and what it does for our lives is essential to walking worthy of the calling we have received as children of God. Do not fall into the prevalent deception that grace is permission to do as you please. Grace turns our hearts away from the world and toward God, but we must grow in that grace to be prepared for the moment when Jesus comes back for His children.

Study Questions

1. What is the relationship between grace and salvation?
   Grace brings salvation; grace bought our salvation.

2. How did you personally experience the saving grace of God?
   Answers will vary.

3. To whom is the gift of salvation offered?
   To all men

4. What does God's grace guide us away from?
   Ungodliness

5. What does God's grace guide us toward?
   A sanctified life

6. In what area(s) has grace led you toward godly living?
   Answers will vary.

7. How will the goodness of grace be demonstrated?
   We have the expectation of Christ; we will see the exaltation of Christ.

8. What prophetic events still need to occur before the Second Coming?
   None

Memory Verses

1 JOHN 3:1–3

1   *Behold, what manner of love the Father hath bestowed upon us, that we should be called the sons of God: therefore the world knoweth us not, because it knew him not.*

2   *Beloved, now are we the sons of God, and it doth not yet appear what we shall be: but we know that, when he shall appear, we shall be like him; for we shall see him as he is.*

3   *And every man that hath this hope in him purifieth himself, even as he is pure.*

A Remembering Grace

Text

HEBREWS 12:14–16

14 Follow peace with all men, and holiness, without which no man shall see the Lord:

15 Looking diligently lest any man fail of the grace of God; lest any root of bitterness springing up trouble you, and thereby many be defiled;

16 Lest there be any fornicator, or profane person, as Esau, who for one morsel of meat sold his birthright.

Overview

Though a Christian can never lose his salvation, every Christian risks failing the grace of God. Forgetting the purpose and power of God's grace places us right in the path of this danger. Every May, our nation sets aside a special Memorial Day to remember those who have given their lives for our freedom. In this same way, we, as Christians, need to specifically and intentionally remember what God has done for us.

In this lesson, we will look at three specific areas of remembrance vital to the Christian life—forgiving, focusing, and fearing the Lord.

Lesson Aim

We want the student to remember what God has done for him, and what He commands him to do in his daily life—a life that can only be lived successfully by His grace.

Lesson Goals

At the conclusion of the lesson, each student should:

1. Grasp the dangers of forgetting God's grace.
2. Be prepared to work on forgiving those who have hurt him.
3. Know the warning signs of bitterness.
4. Focus on his future in Heaven and on Jesus Christ.
5. Understand the true meaning of the fear of the Lord.

Teaching Outline

I. Remember to Forgive.
   A. Forgiveness pursues peace.
   B. Forgiveness defeats bitterness.
      1. Looking diligently
      2. Overcoming bitterness

II. Remember to Focus.
   A. Keep a heavenly focus.
   B. Keep a Christ-centered focus.

III. Remember to Fear.
   A. Remember His voice.
   B. Reverence His commandments.

A Remembering Grace

Text

HEBREWS 12:14–16

14 *Follow peace with all men, and holiness, without which no man shall see the Lord:*

15 *Looking diligently lest any man fail of the grace of God; lest any root of bitterness springing up trouble you, and thereby many be defiled;*

16 *Lest there be any fornicator, or profane person, as Esau, who for one morsel of meat sold his birthright.*

Introduction

Three years after the Civil War ended, Major General Jonathan Logan, commander of the Grand Army of the Republic, issued General Order Number 11 on May 5, 1868. This day was "designated for the purpose of strewing with flowers, or otherwise decorating the graves of comrades who died in defense of their country and during the late rebellion, and whose bodies now lie in almost every city, village, and hamlet churchyard in the land." Originally called Decoration Day, Memorial Day is the day we have set apart to remember those who died valiantly.

In the same way that our country pauses to remember the sacrifices made for our freedom, we are to pause and remember God's grace and the sacrifice Jesus made on our behalf, lest we *"fail of the grace of God."* Please understand that God's grace never fails us, but this passage warns us that, if we do not look to Jesus, we will fail—we will fail to live a life that pleases God, and we will fail to receive the benefits that He has made available to us through grace.

The first-century Hebrew Christians who received this epistle were being enticed to return to the rituals of Judaism rather than standing firmly in grace and resting in the finished work of Jesus Christ. In this passage, they are exhorted to remember God's grace.

I.   Remember to Forgive

HEBREWS 12:14

14   Follow peace with all men, and holiness, without which no man shall see the Lord:

You will never grow in grace if you harbor bitterness in your heart because grace and bitterness are incompatible; they cannot coexist. No doubt, people have wronged you and disappointed you. But no matter what people have done or failed to do, you must forgive. You cannot experience and enjoy the grace of God unless you are willing to forgive.

A. Forgiveness pursues peace.

ROMANS 14:19

19 Let us therefore follow after the things which make for peace, and things wherewith one may edify another.

Bitterness is prevalent in our day. Because it is the tendency of human beings to cling to personal pain rather than to forgive, many are holding grudges from past offenses. Much of society's malaise has at its root this propensity to embrace our own bitterness. Only by His grace can we overcome our fleshly desire for vengeance. Only by His grace can we live at peace with God and with those around us.

God's grace seeks to make peace with others. God did not wait for us to approach Him; Jesus said He came *"to seek and to save that which was lost"* (Luke 19:10). By God's grace, we must take the initiative to forgive those who have offended us, just as Christ took the initiative to forgive. Every relationship in your life needs a forgiver— someone who pursues peace regardless of who is at fault. Take the responsibility to restore the relationship instead of waiting on the other person to make the first move. This pattern is the one Jesus set for us to follow.

If we do not forgive, we will never enjoy the blessings and benefits of peace. A gracious man works to find solutions to live in peace—he follows after *"the things which make for peace."*

B. Forgiveness defeats bitterness.

HEBREWS 12:15–16

15 Looking diligently lest any man fail of the grace of God; lest any root of bitterness springing up trouble you, and thereby many be defiled;

16 Lest there be any fornicator, or profane person, as Esau, who for one morsel of meat sold his birthright.

Bitterness will defile and impoverish your soul. Someone said, "Bitterness is a poison that destroys only the vessel that holds it." Your bitterness against another person will not damage them; in fact, they may never even be aware of it, but it will have long-lasting negative effects on you physically, emotionally, and spiritually.

1. LOOKING DILIGENTLY

Notice the instruction in Hebrews 12:15. We are to look diligently for any bitterness in our lives. The reason bitterness requires such diligence is that it is a hidden problem. The Bible refers to it as a root, something that is buried out of sight. Because our hearts are so deceitful, we are often blind to our own bitterness and its devastation. Undetected, it is an insidious enemy that will grow, reaching into every area of our lives to rob us of the riches of God's grace. Ask God to reveal any bitterness in your heart and to give you the grace to forgive. Forgiveness is the only way to loosen the grasp of this formidable foe.

Illustration

Bruce Goodrich had been accepted into Texas A&M University and was being initiated into the cadet corps at the university. As part of the initiation process, Bruce was taken to the track and told to run until he dropped. He did, but Bruce never got up. Bruce Goodrich died before he even attended his first college class.

A short time after the tragedy, Bruce's father wrote this letter to the administration, faculty, student body, and the corps of cadets: "I would like to take this opportunity to express the appreciation of my family for the great outpouring of concern and sympathy from Texas A&M University and the college community over the loss of our son Bruce. We were deeply touched by the tribute paid to him in the battalion. We were particularly pleased to note that his Christian witness did not go unnoticed during his brief time on campus."

Mr. Goodrich went on: "I hope it will be some comfort to know that we harbor no ill will in the matter. We know our God makes no mistakes. Bruce had an appointment with his Lord and is now secure in his celestial home. When the question is asked, 'Why did this happen?' perhaps one answer will be, 'So that many will consider where they will spend eternity.'" Forgiveness kept the Goodrich family from being destroyed by bitterness though they had suffered a great tragedy.

2.   OVERCOMING BITTERNESS
EPHESIANS 4:30–32
30   And grieve not the holy Spirit of God, whereby ye are sealed unto the day of redemption.
31   Let all bitterness, and wrath, and anger, and clamour, and evil speaking, be put away from you, with all malice:
32   And be ye kind one to another, tenderhearted, forgiving one another, even as God for Christ's sake hath forgiven you.

Why are we to overcome bitterness and forgive others? Our stubborn attachment to our bitterness and our refusal to forgive grieves the heart of God. When we cannot find it in our hearts to forgive the sins of others, we are building a wall between the offender and us; sadly, the same wall separates us from God. Refusing to forgive is an abominable sin in the eyes of God, who has lovingly and mercifully forgiven us of so much.

We have done nothing to merit the forgiveness God extended to us through grace, but because of Jesus' sacrifice on the Cross, we received it nonetheless. No mistreatment you or I have received matches the wickedness that cost Jesus His life, and if God can forgive us for that, we can forgive others no matter what they have done.

We have learned that bitterness lies buried in the dark recesses of our hearts where it thrives and grows and that it is our tendency to conceal it, even to nurture it. How then do we conquer such a stronghold?

2 PETER 3:18

18 But grow in grace, and in the knowledge of our Lord and Saviour Jesus Christ. To him be glory both now and for ever. Amen.

How can you keep a root of bitterness from defiling your faith? Grow in grace. You cannot overcome this enemy on your own, but God has enough grace for whatever trial, burden, injustice, hurt, or tragedy you face. Surrender your wounded spirit to God, and find help in His Word. The grace that God gives when you surrender your brokenness and fill your heart with His Word will help you to let go of the bitterness that controls you.

PROVERBS 4:23

23 Keep thy heart with all diligence; for out of it are the issues of life.

Guarding your heart is critically important. If you do not guard against bitterness, the inevitable trials and difficulties of life will give inroads to Satan's insidious device.

Our text uses Esau as an example of a person profaned by bitterness. Esau had suffered grievous losses. His brother Jacob duped him into giving up his birthright, then cheated him out of his blessing. But the loss of the birthright and the blessing was not Esau's problem; it was the bitterness over these losses that destroyed his relationships with his family and his God.

MATTHEW 7:16–17
16   Ye shall know them by their fruits. Do men gather grapes of thorns, or figs of thistles?
17   Even so every good tree bringeth forth good fruit; but a corrupt tree bringeth forth evil fruit.

A bitter heart will not bring forth fruits of grace. Remember that bitterness and grace cannot coexist in your life. One will drive out the other.

II. Remember to Focus

HEBREWS 12:18, 22
18   For ye are not come unto the mount that might be touched, and that burned with fire, nor unto blackness, and darkness, and tempest,
22   But ye are come unto mount Sion, and unto the city of the living God, the heavenly Jerusalem, and to an innumerable company of angels,

The story of the Exodus from Egypt to the Promised Land was well known to the Hebrew Christians. They had grown up hearing about God's giving the Law to His people at Mount Sinai. This passage draws a contrast between Mount Sinai, where the law was given, and Mount Zion, the symbol of grace. Let's look at where this contrast tells us to place our focus.

A. *Keep a heavenly focus.*

What an awful, fearsome place the foot of Mount Sinai must have been. If anyone trespassed the boundary and touched it, they died. It burned with fire, and darkness and tempest surrounded the peak. The blast of the trumpet and the voice of God sounded so terribly that the people wished to hear them no more. It was a staggering display of the holiness of God Almighty. But the Law is not our focus today. Now we are in the age of grace, and a new heavenly city will be our eternal home. That is where our focus should be.

Physically, Mount Zion is Jerusalem.

PSALM 48:1–3

1 Great is the LORD, and greatly to be praised in the city of our God, in the mountain of his holiness.
2 Beautiful for situation, the joy of the whole earth, is mount Zion, on the sides of the north, the city of the great King.
3 God is known in her palaces for a refuge.

Spiritually, Mount Zion represents the New Jerusalem.

REVELATION 3:12

12 Him that overcometh will I make a pillar in the temple of my God, and he shall go no more out: and I will write upon him the name of my God, and the name of the city of my God, which is new Jerusalem, which cometh down out of heaven from my God: and I will write upon him my new name.

REVELATION 21:2

2 And I John saw the holy city, new Jerusalem, coming down from God out of heaven, prepared as a bride adorned for her husband.

When we are not focused on Heaven, we will not be growing in grace. Rather than the terror and trembling of Mount Sinai, intimate fellowship with God for all eternity is what we look forward to. Because Jesus paid the price for us to enjoy that relationship, we can focus on what bliss lies ahead. This deliberate focus makes earthly trials seem less significant and helps us to trust and remain faithful when difficulties come our way.

B. Keep a Christ-centered focus.

HEBREWS 12:23–24

23 To the general assembly and church of the firstborn, which are written in heaven, and to God the Judge of all, and to the spirits of just men made perfect,
24 And to Jesus the mediator of the new covenant, and to the blood of sprinkling, that speaketh better things than that of Abel.

Both covenants were sealed by blood. The old covenant was sealed by the blood of animals that could not take away sins (Hebrews 10:1–4). The new covenant was sealed by the perfect blood of the Lamb of God that *"taketh away the sin of the world"* (John 1:29). The blood that He shed on the Cross is still speaking today. It *"speaketh better things."* In theological terms this is called efficacy—the blood is just as effective today as it was on the day of the crucifixion, rendering grace to everyone who has trusted in its power.

More than anything else, we need to focus on Jesus, for *"grace and truth came by Jesus Christ"* (John 1:17). The greatest truth about Heaven is not that it is a place where believers will one day gather; the greatest truth is that Jesus will be there. His presence here makes our earthly trials bearable, and the anticipation of His presence in Heaven gives us the hope of blessings and rest prepared for our enjoyment and reward. The great Puritan pastor Richard Baxter expressed his thoughts about this blessed hope in these lines:

> My knowledge of that life is small,
> The eye of faith is dim,
> But it's enough that Christ knows all,
> And I shall be with him.

REVELATION 19:7
7 Let us be glad and rejoice, and give honour to him: for the marriage of the Lamb is come, and his wife hath made herself ready.

TEACHING TIP

Talk to your class about the preparations they made for their weddings. Encourage each student to share a story. Compare the interest and effort we put into preparing for that special day with the preparations we should be making for the day when we see Jesus. Talk about the embarrassment of not being ready for that day, and what it means to truly "love His appearing." Point out that Jesus has been preparing for us (John 14:1–3), and encourage your students to be as diligent in preparing for His return.

III. Remember to Fear

HEBREWS 12:25–29

25 See that ye refuse not him that speaketh. For if they escaped not who refused him that spake on earth, much more shall not we escape, if we turn away from him that speaketh from heaven:

26 Whose voice then shook the earth: but now he hath promised, saying, Yet once more I shake not the earth only, but also heaven.

27 And this word, Yet once more, signifieth the removing of those things that are shaken, as of things that are made, that those things which cannot be shaken may remain.

28 Wherefore we receiving a kingdom which cannot be moved, let us have grace, whereby we may serve God acceptably with reverence and godly fear:

29 For our God is a consuming fire.

In today's society it is no longer popular to talk about fearing God. That message is incongruous with the more popular messages of self-esteem and self-importance. Too many people treat God as a member of the club, the "Man upstairs." But our ignorance and foolhardiness do not change who God is or how we should approach Him.

We looked earlier at the giving of the Law at Mount Sinai and what a fearsome experience it was to behold the awesome display of God's holiness. Though God loves us with an immeasurable, unfathomable love, He abhors sin vehemently and will not allow it to go unpunished. We must live our lives with a biblical understanding of God's holiness.

To fear God is to respect and revere Him. He is *"high and lifted up"* (Isaiah 6:1) and so far above our standard of holiness that there is no way to measure the distance between Him and us. Our very existence rests in the palm of His hand. He is worthy of our reverence and respect. When He convicts us of sin, we must respond to His loving direction rather than rebel and continue on our own course of destruction.

PSALM 89:7

7   God is greatly to be feared in the assembly of the saints, and to be had in reverence of all them that are about him.

Very little reverence or respect is shown in our society today. Parental authority is routinely mocked in entertainment. Government officials are the target for jokes. People no longer respect the house of God or Sunday as a day set apart to worship God. But Christians are not to follow society; we are to follow Scripture, and the Word commands us to revere and fear God.

A. Remember His voice.

HEBREWS 1:1–2

1   God, who at sundry times and in divers manners spake in time past unto the fathers by the prophets,

2   Hath in these last days spoken unto us by his Son, whom he hath appointed heir of all things, by whom also he made the worlds.

What an amazing thought that the God of Heaven would speak to us! He spoke to His children in the past, and He is still speaking to us today. Through His Spirit and His Word, He guides us to do right and to refuse wrong. Some people view the Bible as an ancient book, irrelevant for today's challenges. Nothing could be further from the truth. The only way to know the will and purpose of God for your life is by learning His commands and principles from the Scriptures and listening to the prompting of the Holy Spirit. The Bible has everything you need to live a godly life (2 Peter 1:3).

Hebrews 12 tells us that God shook Mount Sinai because the people were not listening to His voice. How much greater is our responsibility to His Word today? We have the Bible and the Holy Spirit. Every time God speaks to you through preaching, teaching, or the reading of His Word, you must respond in obedience. A good quote to remember: "The only time to do the right thing is right away."

B. *Reverence His commandments.*

2 CORINTHIANS 5:11

11 *Knowing therefore the terror of the Lord, we persuade men; but we are made manifest unto God; and I trust also are made manifest in your consciences.*

A philosophy pervading our society asserts that, because we are under grace, we can live any way we want. This perverted teaching conforms to what people want rather than what the Word says. The fear of the Lord and obedience to Him are not just Old Testament concepts; they are New Testament concepts as well. Hebrews 12:28 instructs us to have grace so that we may acceptably serve and fear God.

Any type of "grace" that teaches you to do less for God or to live a less holy life is fraudulently robbing you of God's blessings on your life. Grace is not a license to ignore the holy commandments of God. No Christian who is genuinely growing in grace is looking for an excuse to do less; he wants to do more for the God who lavishes him with grace.

Illustration

In his sermon *The Allegories of Sarah and Hagar,* Charles Spurgeon said, "What is God's law now? It is not *above* a Christian—it is *under* a Christian. Some men hold God's law like a rod over Christians and say 'If you sin you will be punished with it.' It is not so. The law is under a Christian; it is for him to walk on, to be his guide, his rule, his pattern. Law is the road which guides us, not the rod which drives us nor the spirit which actuates us. The law is good and excellent, if it keeps its place."

1 PETER 4:17–18

17 For the time is come that judgment must begin at the house of God: and if it first begin at us, what shall the end be of them that obey not the gospel of God?
18 And if the righteous scarcely be saved, where shall the ungodly and the sinner appear?

Jesus was *"full of grace and truth"* (John 1:14). In John 8, we witness this balance demonstrated when the scribes and Pharisees brought before Jesus a woman taken in adultery. He said, *"Neither do I condemn thee,"* but He also said, *"go, and sin no more"* (John 8:11). He graciously loves us, but He is also the judge before whom we shall stand one day to give account of our lives (Romans 14:10). We are to live in the awareness of His holiness and practice the reality of His presence. We are not to trample His grace but to grow in it instead.

Conclusion

On May 30, 1868, in response to General Logan's order, volunteers and veterans gathered to place flowers on the graves of both Union and Confederate soldiers buried at Arlington National Cemetery. They did not want the memory of those who had fallen in battle to be forgotten. The greatest sacrifice of all time is the death of Jesus Christ on the Cross where He won the victory in the battle for our salvation. And we must never forget the grace God has bestowed upon us.

Hebrews 12 reminds us of three specific truths. First, we must forgive our enemies so that we do not fall prey to bitterness. Second, we must focus on Jesus Christ and His blessings to us in this life and the life to come. Finally, we must fear God, separating ourselves from a society that refuses to reverence Him.

Study Questions

1. How does remembering to forgive protect us from bitterness?
   Forgiveness pursues peace; forgiveness defeats bitterness.

2. Why must we look diligently for bitterness in our lives?
   Bitterness, like a root, is hidden out of sight.

3. What truth did we learn about the divergence of bitterness and grace?
   They cannot coexist in the same heart.

4. Where is our focus supposed to be?
   On Heaven; on Jesus Christ

5. Besides Jesus, whom are you looking forward to seeing again in Heaven?
   Answers will vary.

6. What does it mean to fear the Lord?
   To reverence and respect a holy God

7. How do we demonstrate our fear of the Lord?
   Remember His voice; reverence His commandments.

8. What grace has God shown in your life that you would like to remember and share?
   Answers will vary.

Memory Verses

HEBREWS 12:14–15

14 *Follow peace with all men, and holiness, without which no man shall see the Lord:*

15 *Looking diligently lest any man fail of the grace of God; lest any root of bitterness springing up trouble you, and thereby many be defiled;*

A Rewarding Grace

Text

ACTS 4:32–37

32 And the multitude of them that believed were of one heart and of one soul: neither said any of them that ought of the things which he possessed was his own; but they had all things common.

33 And with great power gave the apostles witness of the resurrection of the Lord Jesus: and great grace was upon them all.

34 Neither was there any among them that lacked: for as many as were possessors of lands or houses sold them, and brought the prices of the things that were sold,

35 And laid them down at the apostles' feet: and distribution was made unto every man according as he had need.

36 And Joses, who by the apostles was surnamed Barnabas, (which is, being interpreted, The son of consolation,) a Levite, and of the country of Cyprus,

37 Having land, sold it, and brought the money, and laid it at the apostles' feet.

Overview

The early church was characterized by the presence of God's Spirit and grace. "Great grace" was manifested in their relationships, their giving, and their witness. The reason the church is not impacting the world as it should is that we lack the grace we read about in this passage.

God bestowed grace upon this early church to do His work, and in turn, He blessed them for their faithful service. In this lesson, we will study three areas on which God showered His blessing—gracious spirits, generous stewardship, and great soulwinning.

Lesson Aim

We want the students to understand that as members of a grace-filled church they have a role in helping the church fulfill its purpose and calling.

Lesson Goals

At the conclusion of the lesson, each student should:

1. Know the characteristics of a grace-filled church.
2. Grasp the importance of a gracious spirit.
3. Have a Bible-based philosophy of giving.
4. Focus on his responsibility and privilege to win souls.
5. See every person as an eternal soul who needs salvation.

Teaching Outline

I. Gracious in Their Spirit
   A. They were of one faith.
      1. They had faith in Christ.
      2. They had fellowship in Christ.
   B. They were of one heart.
      1. They were one in Christ.
      2. They were one for Christ.
   C. They were of one soul.

II. Generous in Their Stewardship
   A. The believers were unselfish.
   B. The believers were sacrificial.

III. Great in Their Soulwinning
- A. Powerful witness
  1. Power in the messengers
  2. Power in the message
- B. Proven witness
  1. Proven by the Resurrection
  2. Proven by changed lives

A Rewarding Grace

Text

ACTS 4:32–37

32 And the multitude of them that believed were of one heart and of one soul: neither said any of them that ought of the things which he possessed was his own; but they had all things common.

33 And with great power gave the apostles witness of the resurrection of the Lord Jesus: and great grace was upon them all.

34 Neither was there any among them that lacked: for as many as were possessors of lands or houses sold them, and brought the prices of the things that were sold,

35 And laid them down at the apostles' feet: and distribution was made unto every man according as he had need.

36 And Joses, who by the apostles was surnamed Barnabas, (which is, being interpreted, The son of consolation,) a Levite, and of the country of Cyprus,

37 Having land, sold it, and brought the money, and laid it at the apostles' feet.

Introduction

Perhaps no other church in history has experienced the grace of God and His presence and power to the extent that the church in Jerusalem experienced it. Over 3,000 people were saved, baptized, and added to the church on the day of Pentecost alone.

ACTS 2:41
41 Then they that gladly received his word were baptized: and the same day there were added unto them about three thousand souls.

Our text describes that church as having *"great grace."* Grace is not something that can be duplicated in the power of the flesh; it is a disposition created in our lives by the Holy Spirit of God. It is a gift of God that brings rich rewards into our lives through its presence.

As a result of the grace God bestowed upon the early Christians, each part of their lives was changed. The way that they interacted with each other, the way they gave, and the way they witnessed were all dramatically impacted by the presence of God's grace. Grace is not a theoretical concept; it is a practical, daily, life-changing gift of God. Grace outwardly evidences God's hand in your life so that others can see grace when they look at you.

I.   Gracious in Their Spirit

Because grace is God's inward work, it first renews our spirits, then manifests itself outwardly in our works. A unified spirit characterized the church in Jerusalem. These people were just like us; things went wrong between them, but rather than react in selfishness and anger, they responded in grace, resolving their differences and maintaining harmony within the church. This unity was not manufactured; it was produced by grace.

A. They were of one faith.

The leaders of the church, the apostles, had spent years walking with Christ and learning from Him, and they studied the Scriptures to verify for others that His life, death, and resurrection were those foretold by the prophets. These people came from all walks of life and from many different countries, but one thing brought them together—they all had the same faith.

1. THEY HAD FAITH IN CHRIST.

ACTS 4:10–12

10 *Be it known unto you all, and to all the people of Israel, that by the name of Jesus Christ of Nazareth, whom ye crucified, whom God raised from the dead, even by him doth this man stand here before you whole.*

11 *This is the stone which was set at nought of you builders, which is become the head of the corner.*

12 *Neither is there salvation in any other: for there is none other name under heaven given among men, whereby we must be saved.*

The members of that church had a common belief centered on the person of Jesus Christ.

The hymn writer called this faith "the tie that binds our hearts in Christian love." There is a level and depth of unity that can exist only among believers. Because we have the same Holy Spirit living within us, we have something in common that is more important than anything that could divide us.

2. THEY HAD FELLOWSHIP IN CHRIST.

ACTS 2:42

42   And they continued stedfastly in the apostles' doctrine and fellowship, and in breaking of bread, and in prayers.

The only basis for true fellowship is doctrine. Many churches today ignore doctrine to facilitate fellowship, but if we do not have the same basic beliefs, we will never be able to have the kind of unity and fellowship that the Bible describes. Those who ignore the doctrine of Christ can have a religious gathering, but they have nothing of grace in their so-called fellowship. Amos 3:3 teaches that we cannot walk together unless we are in agreement.

B. They were of one heart.

The word *heart* used in the text is referring to feelings and emotions. The church in Jerusalem had unity because they shared a love for Jesus Christ. Their hearts were focused on the same great love, which bound them together.

1. THEY WERE ONE IN CHRIST.

JOHN 17:11

11   And now I am no more in the world, but these are in the world, and I come to thee. Holy Father, keep through thine own name those whom thou hast given me, that they may be one, as we are.

Jesus prayed that His people would experience unity in the same way that He and His Father shared perfect harmony and unity. But unity is not a goal worth reaching at any cost. Charles Spurgeon said, "Unity without truth is hazardous." Real unity is produced as a byproduct of shared commitment to the truth. The church had unity based on their shared relationship with Jesus Christ and the teaching they received from the apostles.

2. THEY WERE ONE FOR CHRIST.

People from many different nations had come to Jerusalem to celebrate the Passover. Many of them had remained during the Feast of Unleavened Bread, waiting for the Day of Pentecost. On that day, they heard Peter preach in the power of the Holy Spirit, and more than 3,000 were saved.

ACTS 2:9–11

9 *Parthians, and Medes, and Elamites, and the dwellers in Mesopotamia, and in Judaea, and Cappadocia, in Pontus, and Asia,*

10 *Phrygia, and Pamphylia, in Egypt, and in the parts of Libya about Cyrene, and strangers of Rome, Jews and proselytes,*

11 *Cretes and Arabians, we do hear them speak in our tongues the wonderful works of God.*

They had different backgrounds and languages, different customs and cultures, but they were united by a common cause—sharing God's love. Healing for racial division and prejudice cannot be produced by political or social programs; the love of God begins this healing in the hearts of people who have been born again. When people are drawn to the Gospel and trust Christ as Saviour, they find a purpose that draws them together no matter how they differ.

C. They were of one soul.

The soul is often spoken of as our personality, our inherent strengths and weaknesses or those we develop over time. These early Christians were united by a love for Jesus that created in them a desire to serve Him. This desire brought them together to form a body in which each person used his own personal strengths to get God's work done.

The friendship that developed between David and Jonathan is an example of different personalities uniting. Their unity was produced, not because they had the same personality type—no two people could have been more different—but because their souls had like passions.

1 SAMUEL 18:1

1 And it came to pass, when he had made an end of speaking unto Saul, that the soul of Jonathan was knit with the soul of David, and Jonathan loved him as his own soul.

There is no unity apart from the grace of God. Today we need a revival of graciousness among Christians. Churches are suffering from divisions, even trivial divisions such as which hymnbook to purchase or what color of carpet to buy. With God's grace, we should set aside personality differences and personal preferences to focus on the work that needs to be done.

TEACHING TIP

Focus on the concept of unity as a byproduct of shared faith and purpose rather than a goal to be pursued at any cost. You may want to use a sports metaphor to illustrate this truth. The crowd at a football game includes thousands of people from very different backgrounds, economic and education levels, and ethnicity. But their differences are immaterial because of their shared commitment to cheer their team to victory. If we love Jesus and the truths He's given us the way we should, that love will overwhelm anything else that might divide us.

II. Generous in Their Stewardship

Generosity is not a natural human trait. We tend to be selfish, trying to get all we can and keep all we get. But the members in the church at Jerusalem did not look at their possessions as something to be held tightly. In fact, they didn't even regard their possessions as their own. They recognized the core truth of all stewardship—that God owns everything we have; we are just stewards managing what He has entrusted to our care.

A. *The believers were unselfish.*

Their attitude was, "If I can help you with anything that I have, it's yours." This kind of generosity is not normal. It was a result of the great grace that prevailed in that church. In fact, the New Testament describes giving as a grace.

2 CORINTHIANS 8:7–9

7 Therefore, as ye abound in every thing, in faith, and utterance, and knowledge, and in all diligence, and in your love to us, see that ye abound in this grace also.

8 I speak not by commandment, but by occasion of the forwardness of others, and to prove the sincerity of your love.

9 For ye know the grace of our Lord Jesus Christ, that, though he was rich, yet for your sakes he became poor, that ye through his poverty might be rich.

Old Testament giving was bound by a percentage of income. New Testament giving is proportionate to what God has given us. If we Christians were to yield to the Holy Spirit's leading, He would direct us in our giving, and God's work would never suffer need. A church that has great grace will not have puny giving. Setting a good example in giving is a legacy we must pass on to our children as well.

Illustration

A little boy was sitting in church with his family for the first time. He was interested in everything he saw because it was all new to him. When they took the offering, he watched the ushers moving from row to row, passing the offering plates. He tugged on his father's coat sleeve and said, "You don't have to pay for me, Daddy, I'm under five!"

B. The believers were sacrificial.

The giving in the church at Jerusalem was a response to the great needs they were experiencing. These Christians were even willing to sell houses and land to meet the needs of the church. This kind of sacrifice is not usually required of us, but it is something that we should be willing to offer. Because every good thing that we have is a gift from God, He is ultimately the owner of all that we possess. The resources that He has given to us are to be used for His work and to help meet the needs of others.

1 TIMOTHY 6:17–18

17 Charge them that are rich in this world, that they be not highminded, nor trust in uncertain riches, but in the living God, who giveth us richly all things to enjoy;
18 That they do good, that they be rich in good works, ready to distribute, willing to communicate;

God wants us to enjoy the blessings that He has freely given to us, but he also wants us to be "ready to distribute."

We are not to become attached to our possessions. Giving is at the very heart of Christianity—God gave His only begotten Son because of His love for us. Statistics tell us that in most churches twenty percent of the people give eighty percent of the money. That is not the mark of a grace-filled church.

III. Great in Their Soulwinning

This church had great grace. Being filled with the Holy Spirit, they never went anywhere without telling someone about the Lord Jesus Christ. Although it is a good thing to have a regularly scheduled soulwinning time, we also need to be alert to opportunities to witness every day. Every person you meet is destined to spend eternity either in Heaven with God or in Hell without Him, and that reality enjoins on us an awesome responsibility to tell each one the truth before it is too late.

A. Powerful witness

The Bible tells us that the members of the church at Jerusalem had great power as they shared the Gospel with others. We must have that power if our witnessing is to be effective. We do not win souls—the Holy Spirit wins men and women- -but we need His power in the message we present. Our feeble words apart from His power will fall to the ground.

1. POWER IN THE MESSENGERS

ACTS 1:8

8   *But ye shall receive power, after that the Holy Ghost is come upon you: and ye shall be witnesses unto me both in*

Jerusalem, and in all Judaea, and in Samaria, and unto the uttermost part of the earth.

1 Thessalonians 1:5
5   *For our gospel came not unto you in word only, but also in power, and in the Holy Ghost, and in much assurance; as ye know what manner of men we were among you for your sake.*

Many churches are changing their methods of soulwinning today because they are not seeing the results they wish to see. The problem is not the method. The method Jesus gave to His disciples is perfectly effective today—that is if we carry it out in His power as they did. The church does not need new tactics and techniques, the church needs a new touch of the Holy Spirit's power, for He is the only one who can produce a real and lasting harvest.

2.   Power in the message
Romans 1:16
16   *For I am not ashamed of the gospel of Christ: for it is the power of God unto salvation to every one that believeth; to the Jew first, and also to the Greek.*

The word *power* in Greek is *dunamis*, from which we get our word *dynamite*. The Gospel of Christ is a powerful message. Just as we do not need different methods for reaching our world, we also do not need an updated message. The "old, old story of Jesus and His love" is exactly what our world needs to hear today. A powerful messenger delivering a powerful message will see powerful results. God will use you to bring others to Jesus Christ if you are walking in the fullness and power of the Holy Spirit.

B. *Proven witness*

When someone is called as a witness in court, his words are compared against the evidence that has been presented. When you are a witness for Christ, your words are not unsubstantiated—you have trustworthy evidence attesting to the truth. Jesus' resurrection from the dead and the lives that have been changed by the Gospel are powerful support for the message you present.

1.   PROVEN BY THE RESURRECTION

1 CORINTHIANS 15:3–8

3   *For I delivered unto you first of all that which I also received, how that Christ died for our sins according to the scriptures;*

4   *And that he was buried, and that he rose again the third day according to the scriptures:*

5   *And that he was seen of Cephas, then of the twelve:*

6   *After that, he was seen of above five hundred brethren at once; of whom the greater part remain unto this present, but some are fallen asleep.*

7   *After that, he was seen of James; then of all the apostles.*

8   *And last of all he was seen of me also, as of one born out of due time.*

Apart from the Resurrection, the message of Christianity has no power or meaning. If Jesus had not risen from the dead, we would have no hope of salvation. The Resurrection is the proof of the Christian faith. It must be a part of our witness. We are not to be ashamed of the Gospel, and the Resurrection is a vital part of that Gospel.

2. PROVEN BY CHANGED LIVES

The grace of God transforms those who believe, and the world has no explanation for lives changed by the power of the Gospel. Such was the case with Lazarus' testimony. After Jesus raised him from the dead, his influence was so powerful that Lazarus became a concern to the Jewish leaders. In fact, they desired to kill Lazarus to silence his compelling testimony.

JOHN 12:9–11

9   Much people of the Jews therefore knew that he was there: and they came not for Jesus' sake only, but that they might see Lazarus also, whom he had raised from the dead.

10   But the chief priests consulted that they might put Lazarus also to death;

11   Because that by reason of him many of the Jews went away, and believed on Jesus.

Your own story of God's grace gives evidence to the truth of the Gospel witness you share with others. The apostle Paul often told the story of his encounter with Jesus on the road to Damascus. He repeated his story, not because he had nothing else to say, but because his conversion could not be explained apart from the power and grace of God.

Conclusion

Years ago, a preacher friend of mine told me that no one is standing still in the Christian life. He said, "Each person is either moving forward or moving backward." The only way that you can move forward as a believer is to grow in the grace of God. God's grace renews your spirit—a renewal which manifests graciousness in your interactions with others. God's grace creates generosity within your heart. And God's grace will produce powerful results as you work to lead people to Jesus.

Nothing that we do successfully for God is done by our own power. Jesus said, *"Without me ye can do nothing"* (John 15:5). All of the credit and glory and praise belong to God alone. Everything we accomplish in our own lives and through our church is because of His great grace.

Study Questions

1. What three elements demonstrated the presence of grace in the church at Jerusalem?
   One faith, one heart, one soul

2. What is the relationship between doctrine and fellowship?
   True fellowship is the result of right doctrine.

3. What evidences of unity have you seen in your church?
   Answers will vary.

4. What two things demonstrated grace in the early church's giving?
   The believers were unselfish; the believers were sacrificial.

5. What does the New Testament call giving?
   A grace

6. What made the early church great in their soulwinning?
   Powerful witness, proven witness

7. Can you share an example of when you have seen the power of the Gospel?
   Answers will vary.

8. What changes in your life point to the power of the Gospel?
   Answers will vary.

Memory Verses

ACTS 4:32–33

32 And the multitude of them that believed were of one heart and of one soul: neither said any of them that ought of the things which he possessed was his own; but they had all things common.

33 And with great power gave the apostles witness of the resurrection of the Lord Jesus: and great grace was upon them all.

A Reviving Grace

Text

1 From whence come wars and fightings among you? come they not hence, even of your lusts that war in your members?

2 Ye lust, and have not: ye kill, and desire to have, and cannot obtain: ye fight and war, yet ye have not, because ye ask not.

3 Ye ask, and receive not, because ye ask amiss, that ye may consume it upon your lusts.

4 Ye adulterers and adulteresses, know ye not that the friendship of the world is enmity with God? whosoever therefore will be a friend of the world is the enemy of God.

5 Do ye think that the scripture saith in vain, The spirit that dwelleth in us lusteth to envy?

6 But he giveth more grace. Wherefore he saith, God resisteth the proud, but giveth grace unto the humble.

7 Submit yourselves therefore to God. Resist the devil, and he will flee from you.

Overview

Every Christian reaches a point where he needs revival in his heart. The world, the flesh, and the devil are constantly working to lure our hearts away from full devotion to God. The sweetness of close fellowship with God that we once enjoyed can be lost a little at a time, almost without our realizing it. In this lesson we are going to examine what revival is, what hinders us from experiencing revival, how it comes to the people of God, and what the results of a genuine revival will be. By presenting the Bible model of revival, we will also equip our students to discern the allurements that draw some people away from the Lord.

Lesson Aim

We want the students to understand the role that grace plays in bringing revival to their own lives and into the church at large, and we want to create a desire in them for such a reviving of grace.

Lesson Goals

At the conclusion of the lesson, each student should:

1. See the need for personal and corporate revival.
2. Recognize the conflicts that prevent revival.
3. Know how to avoid the things that compete with true revival.
4. Understand the implications of experiencing revival.
5. Have a heart desire to see revival come.

Teaching Outline

    I. The Conflicts with Revival
       A. Conflict with strife
          1. Fighting in the flesh
          2. Not walking in the Spirit
       B. Conflict with selfishness
          1. The process of selfishness
          2. The product of selfishness

II. The Competition for Revival
   A. Misplaced prayer
   B. Misplaced values
   C. Misplaced friendship

III. The Commencement of Revival
   A. Revival begins with a contrite heart.
   B. Revival develops a conformed heart.
      1. A humble heart submits to God's leading.
      2. A humble heart resists the devil.

A Reviving Grace

Text

JAMES 4:1–7

1   From whence come wars and fightings among you? come they not hence, even of your lusts that war in your members?

2   Ye lust, and have not: ye kill, and desire to have, and cannot obtain: ye fight and war, yet ye have not, because ye ask not.

3   Ye ask, and receive not, because ye ask amiss, that ye may consume it upon your lusts.

4   Ye adulterers and adulteresses, know ye not that the friendship of the world is enmity with God? whosoever therefore will be a friend of the world is the enemy of God.

5   Do ye think that the scripture saith in vain, The spirit that dwelleth in us lusteth to envy?

6   But he giveth more grace. Wherefore he saith, God resisteth the proud, but giveth grace unto the humble.

7   Submit yourselves therefore to God. Resist the devil, and he will flee from you.

Introduction

Every Christian comes to the point in his life, usually more than once, where he needs a work of grace to rekindle in his heart the passion he once had for God. The things from the Word of God that once stirred him are no longer of interest. Little things that he would have overlooked before now cause irritation or frustration. The love for the Lord that once was fervent has cooled.

When this happens, when the love has grown cold and the joy is gone, we need revival. In Psalm 85:6, the psalmist expresses Israel's need for revival: *"Wilt thou not revive us again: that thy people may rejoice in thee?"* Vance Havner said, "Revival is the church falling in love with Jesus all over again." Revival restores the joy of your salvation, the way you felt the moment you were saved.

Revival is not something that is confined to a scheduled time. You don't have to wait for a guest speaker or a week of special meetings to experience the renewing and reviving work of grace in your heart and life. And if your heart has grown cold and you have allowed sin to linger in your life, you need revival now.

Illustration

I heard about a little boy who got up one morning and went into the kitchen for his breakfast. His mother was shocked to see that he was covered in dirt from head to foot. She asked, "How did you get so dirty so early in the morning?"

"Oh Mom, that was easy," he said. "I went to bed this way!"

I. The Conflicts with Revival

JAMES 3:14–16

14 *But if ye have bitter envying and strife in your hearts, glory not, and lie not against the truth.*
15 *This wisdom descendeth not from above, but is earthly, sensual, devilish.*
16 *For where envying and strife is, there is confusion and every evil work.*

Revival does not come automatically, nor is it guaranteed. And if you really desire revival in your own life and in your church, conflict and opposition will arise. The devil does not want your love for God to be renewed, and he will do everything in his power to prevent restoration. Though believers have the Holy Spirit living within them and possess a new nature, they will still face conflict, especially when they need revival.

A. Conflict with strife

The first conflict is an inward problem. James says conflict comes from "your lusts." Our desires war against the work that God wants to do in our lives. We have been regenerated through salvation, but the old nature and its desires remain. The fleshly nature is constantly at war against the Spirit living within us. As a result, the unity that is supposed to characterize the body of Christ is often broken.

PSALM 133:1

1 *Behold, how good and how pleasant it is for brethren to dwell together in unity!*

The churches who received this letter from James were experiencing great persecution. Many faced imprisonment or lost their jobs or even their lives for their faith. The frustration that they felt because of hardship was spilling over into their relationships within the church.

If there is strife in your heart, it is going to come out and cause strife within the church. Someone who has resentment and hostility in his own soul is going to see it manifested in conflicts.

1. FIGHTING IN THE FLESH

Thus, in the one place where they should have been most able to expect fellowship and encouragement, the Christians in James 3 found contention instead. In the phrase "wars and fightings among you" the words *among you* indicate that these contentious relationships involved members of the churches. Also in the text, the Greek word used for wars is polemos, from which we get the word polemic. Polemic means "of or involving dispute; controversial, argumentative." What a sad description of these Christians' lives.

When your heart is not right with God, you will find it very easy to get frustrated and angry. The simplest statement can trigger a strong reaction and strife. Christians experiencing this kind of discord need revival.

2. NOT WALKING IN THE SPIRIT

GALATIANS 5:16–18

16 *This I say then, Walk in the Spirit, and ye shall not fulfill the lust of the flesh.*

17 *For the flesh lusteth against the Spirit, and the Spirit against the flesh: and these are contrary the one to the other: so that ye cannot do the things that ye would.*

18   But if ye be led of the Spirit, ye are not under the law.

Fighting and dissension is evidence of walking in the flesh, rather than in the Spirit. These verses in Galatians describe the internal conflict between the Spirit and our flesh, each fighting against the other for control. Both cannot win; one or the other must lose. If you are not walking in the Spirit, you can expect a life filled with conflict.

B.   *Conflict with selfishness*

2 PETER 2:10

10   But chiefly them that walk after the flesh in the lust of uncleanness, and despise government. Presumptuous are they, selfwilled, they are not afraid to speak evil of dignities.

Walking after the flesh produces selfishness. When we are in the flesh, we tend to focus more and more on what we want, creating a vicious cycle. As James noted, first people are driven by their desires, then they lose control, and eventually the desires take control of them. The references James makes to lust and desire are red flag warnings of selfishness.

1.   THE PROCESS OF SELFISHNESS

The people to whom James was writing were driven by the "desire to have"—a phrase indicating a burning, zealous desire. The selfishness they allowed into their lives took them further and further away from God and made them miserable because they were not getting the things they wanted. Marital conflicts, family conflicts, job conflicts, national conflicts—all these are the result of unsatisfied lust and envying. Remember, the word *lusts* does not necessarily mean sensual passions; it simply means a strong desire.

2. THE PRODUCT OF SELFISHNESS

Selfishness is not a "victimless crime." Just because it starts on the inside does not mean it stays there. The danger of selfishness is that a selfish person is never satisfied. Getting what we want doesn't satisfy us; it makes us want still more. Selfishness became so strong that James said, "ye kill." I don't believe that is primarily referencing murder, although certainly that can happen in extreme cases. But selfishness can kill relationships, kill opportunities to serve others, and kill the Lord's work. Selfishness makes us complacent toward spiritual things because our focus is on feeding our fleshly desires. Second Peter 2:17–21 describes the end of these self-willed people we read about in verse 10 and the tragic effect they have on others:

2 PETER 2:17–21

17   These are wells without water, clouds that are carried with a tempest; to whom the mist of darkness is reserved for ever.

18   For when they speak great swelling words of vanity, they allure through the lusts of the flesh, through much wantonness, those that were clean escaped from them who live in error.

19   While they promise them liberty, they themselves are the servants of corruption: for of whom a man is overcome, of the same is he brought in bondage.

20   For if after they have escaped the pollutions of the world through the knowledge of the Lord and Saviour Jesus

Christ, they are again entangled therein, and overcome, the latter end is worse with them than the beginning.

21 For it had been better for them not to have known the way of righteousness, than, after they have known it, to turn from the holy commandment delivered unto them.

The presence of selfishness is a strong indicator that we need revival.

Illustration

I read that a lady approached the famous evangelist Billy Sunday and asked him, "Why do you keep having revival meetings? Don't you realize that the results only last a little while?"

"Why do you keep taking baths?" Sunday asked.

Selfishness will creep into our lives again and again. We need revival to purge our hearts of selfishness and sin.

II. The Competition for Revival

As we've already seen, the devil does not want you to experience revival. So when revival starts, he is going to work to defeat it and keep you from enjoying the benefits of a renewed relationship with Jesus Christ. There are three specific areas where we will be tempted to trade a genuine relationship with God for a substitute.

A. *Misplaced prayer*

Revival does not come aside from praying for it with a pure heart. But James said that some prayers are not answered because we "ask amiss." The Greek word used here is *kakos*, meaning "miserable, improper or sick." When our prayers are wrong, based on evil or selfishness, there will be no revival. Instead of praying for God to weigh our desires and being willing to repent and forsake them if they are not in God's will, we often ask for our desires to be granted so that we can have more pleasure rather than glorify Him.

Before we ask for something, we need to make sure our hearts are right in asking. If you have been saved for a while, you would probably join me in saying you're glad that God didn't answer all of your prayers. In my flesh, I've asked God for some things that could have damaged my life had they been granted. Wrong praying reveals a selfish heart that will preclude revival.

Illustration

A seven-year-old girl won $2.00 for the "quiet prize" in Sunday school. She was telling her parents about it after the service, and they were very happy for her. She said, "I gave it all to Jesus in the offering this morning."

"That's wonderful," her mother said. "I'm sure God will be pleased."

"Yes," the daughter said. "Now maybe God will let me do some of the things I want to do!"

B. Misplaced values

1 JOHN 2:15–16

15 *Love not the world, neither the things that are in the world. If any man love the world, the love of the Father is not in him.*

16 For all that is in the world, the lust of the flesh, and the lust of the eyes, and the pride of life, is not of the Father, but is of the world.

James uses a very blunt metaphor to drive home his point about where our values should be. In the text, he addressed the readers as adulterers and adulteresses. The Bible several times uses adultery to paint a picture of our hearts turning away from God. In the Old Testament, God bound Himself to Israel in a covenant relationship similar to marriage. When Israel fell into idolatry, God referred to their turning away as adultery. Israel committed spiritual unfaithfulness when they went after idols. These strong words should impress upon us the seriousness with which God views our relationship to Him.

Marriage is also used in the New Testament to picture the relationship between Christ and the church. Jesus purchased the church, His bride, through the shedding of His blood on the Cross. As we stray from love for Him, it is a grievous betrayal.

1 PETER 1:18–19
18 Forasmuch as ye know that ye were not redeemed with corruptible things, as silver and gold, from your vain conversation received by tradition from your fathers;
19 But with the precious blood of Christ, as of a lamb without blemish and without spot:

Illustration

In the Jewish culture, before a couple married, they were betrothed. Betrothal was a legally binding contract to enter into marriage. After the betrothal was arranged, the bridegroom would go away to prepare a place for his bride to live. Then once his father felt that everything was prepared, he would go and claim his bride, bringing her home to live with him.

Right now, the church is in the betrothal period. Jesus is in Heaven preparing a place for each of us (John 14:1–3). While we are here on earth waiting for Him to return, we must separate ourselves unto Christ and from the world. You will face a constant pull from the world to draw away from Jesus, but if we fall in love with the world, we are committing spiritual adultery against Him.

2 Corinthians 11:1–3

1   *Would to God ye could bear with me a little in my folly: and indeed bear with me.*

2   *For I am jealous over you with godly jealousy: for I have espoused you to one husband, that I may present you as a chaste virgin to Christ.*

3   *But I fear, lest by any means, as the serpent beguiled Eve through his subtilty, so your minds should be corrupted from the simplicity that is in Christ.*

Colossians 2:8

8   *Beware lest any man spoil you through philosophy and vain deceit, after the tradition of men, after the rudiments of the world, and not after Christ.*

C. Misplaced friendship

Christians who want to be in a right friendship with God cannot be friends with the world. Again, James leaves no middle ground. Anyone who wants to be a friend of the world is an enemy of our Lord and Saviour, Jesus Christ. World here is *kosmos*, not the physical earth, but the man-centered system in this present age. That this world's system is centered on the fallacy of man's philosophies and reasoning is why James says to befriend the world is to become God's enemy.

God gives us good things to enjoy (1 Timothy 6:17). By telling us not to love and befriend the world, He is not trying to take good things from us; He is telling us to keep Him in His rightful place. God wants to be on the throne of your heart, and as the King of the Universe, He will not settle for less than your full love and devotion. If you want real revival, God must be your very best friend.

> **TEACHING TIP**
>
> *Spend some time with your students talking about the different approaches people have taken to avoid being drawn into friendship with the world. You may want to contrast the monastic approach—where people withdraw from the world completely—with Jesus' example as "the friend of sinners." He spent time with them, ministering to them, while loving His Father supremely. This is a vital balance to maintain. Ask your class to discuss how they have gained or missed opportunities to witness in this context.*

III. The Commencement of Revival

Revival is a work of grace in our hearts and lives. It is not something we produce through our own efforts; true revival can only come from God. It's true that there are obstacles and opposition to revival, but God gives "*more grace*" (James 4:6). Grace is the inner working of the Holy Spirit to give us power to overcome the world and to renew our love for Him. No matter how serious the problems in your life or in your church, there is more than enough grace to produce a revival to overcome them.

A. *Revival begins with a contrite heart.*

Show me a Christian who is frustrated by what he doesn't have or a Christian who is bitter about prayers that haven't been answered, and I will show you a Christian who needs revival but cannot have it until he is willing to humble himself. Sometimes the problem is that God is offering us help, but we want to do things our own way and in our own power.

Illustration

I was sitting in the backyard with my daughter after we had finished setting up for my son's sixteenth birthday party. Beyond the fence, I saw a little puff of smoke. I thought maybe it was due to some construction, but the smoke continued to grow. I decided we needed to go take a look. In the field beyond our yard, a patch of dry grass was burning. It was a small fire then, but the wind was blowing strongly, so we went down the street to warn the neighbors.

When the lady came to the door I said, "Ma'am, there's a fire burning about a quarter mile from your house, but the wind is blowing your way. I just wanted to let you know to watch out for it." By the time she came outside, though only a few minutes had passed, the fire had raced across the field and was at her back yard. She was very worried about her animals, so we went to help her get them out. The flames were leaping up on the stall of a big, black bull. I was trying to get him out to save his life, but he wasn't happy to see me! I tried to lead him, I tried to chase him, I tried everything I could think of, but he wouldn't move. I was trying to show him the way to safety, but he didn't want my help. I thought we were going to have prime rib roast for dinner. Finally, he took off and made it away from the fire.

When we humble our stubborn hearts before the Lord, then He will extend His grace to us. He will do a transforming work in us, and we will know the power and joy of real revival.

PSALM 51:10
10   Create in me a clean heart, O God; and renew a right spirit within me.

JAMES 4:10
10   Humble yourselves in the sight of the Lord, and he shall lift you up.

B. Revival develops a conformed heart.

When revival comes, it does a work in our hearts and changes our direction to bring us another step closer to the image of Jesus Christ. Conforming to His image is God's ultimate purpose for our lives (Romans 8:28–29).

1.   A HUMBLE HEART SUBMITS TO GOD'S LEADING.

It takes humility to submit our hearts so that God can mold us and shape us to the image of Christ. Unless we are willing to humble ourselves to the Lord, we will not be submissive to Him, and we will not receive His grace. The word *submit* in James 4:7 is *hupotasso* which means "to arrange under, to subordinate; to subject, put in subjection; to subject one's self, to obey." It is primarily a military term meaning "to arrange in an orderly fashion under the command of a leader." In non-military use, it indicates "a voluntary attitude of giving in, cooperating, assuming responsibility, and carrying a burden." Are you fighting God? Must He use pressure to cause you to yield to His molding, or do you have a tender, humble heart that is pliable in His hand?

2. A HUMBLE HEART RESISTS THE DEVIL.

The word *resist* is *anthistemi*, meaning "to set one's self against, to withstand, resist, oppose." Once we are in submission to God, we are under a higher authority and power than that which Satan or any of his demons possess. Therefore, by God's power and authority, we are able to resist, withstand, and oppose the devil. Your enemy cannot defeat you without your help. In fact, James says that when we do resist him, he runs away!

Conclusion

James Stewart said, "Revival is the people of God living in the power of an ungrieved, unquenched Spirit." Many churches today are filled with people who are living the Christian life as if they were under bondage. They are not vibrant, victorious, rejoicing Christians; they are discouraged and defeated Christians. They need a work of God's grace to bring revival into their hearts and lives.

God is calling His people today to repentance and revival. He is offering grace to help you defeat your flesh, the world, and the devil. The question is, will you seek His help with a humble, contrite heart?

REVELATION 3:19–20

19 As many as I love, I rebuke and chasten: be zealous therefore, and repent.
20 Behold, I stand at the door, and knock: if any man hear my voice, and open the door, I will come in to him, and will sup with him, and he with me.

Study Questions

1. What are the conflicts that attempt to block revival from our lives?
    Conflict with strife, conflict with selfishness

2. How does selfishness manifest itself in the life of a Christian?
    Answers will vary.

3. What can selfishness kill in our lives?
    Relationships, opportunities to serve, the Lord's work

4. What things can compete with revival for our attention?
    Misplaced prayer, misplaced values, misplaced friendship

5. To what does God compare the process of our hearts being drawn away from Him?
    Adultery

6. How are you striving to be a friend of sinners without being a friend of the world?
    Answers will vary.

7. What relationship does revival have with the condition of our hearts?
    Revival begins with a contrite heart; revival develops a conformed heart.

8. What does God do when our hearts are proud instead of humble?
    Resists us

Memory Verses

1 JOHN 2:15–16

15   Love not the world, neither the things that are in the world. If any man love the world, the love of the Father is not in him. 16   For all that is in the world, the lust of the flesh, and the lust of the eyes, and the pride of life, is not of the Father, but is of the world.

A Reassuring Grace

Text

2 TIMOTHY 1:5–9

5 When I call to remembrance the unfeigned faith that is in thee, which dwelt first in thy grandmother Lois, and thy mother Eunice; and I am persuaded that in thee also.

6 Wherefore I put thee in remembrance that thou stir up the gift of God, which is in thee by the putting on of my hands.

7 For God hath not given us the spirit of fear; but of power, and of love, and of a sound mind.

8 Be not thou therefore ashamed of the testimony of our Lord, nor of me his prisoner: but be thou partaker of the afflictions of the gospel according to the power of God;

9 Who hath saved us, and called us with an holy calling, not according to our works, but according to his own purpose and grace, which was given us in Christ Jesus before the world began,

Overview

We are living in a world of uncertainty and doubt. Many people are struggling with the pressures and fears they face to the point that some of the best-selling prescription drugs in America are depression and anxiety treatments. But God has the best answer for His children—He offers us His grace.

In this lesson, we will study the role that grace plays in giving us assurance and confidence during difficult times. We will look at the promise of God to provide us with power, love, and a sound mind. The same grace that helped the Apostle Paul through great persecution, suffering, and even martyrdom is available to us today.

Lesson Aim

We want the students to learn how, through the grace of God, to exchange a life filled with fear, dread, and doubt for a life of power, of love, and of a sound mind.

Lesson Goals

At the conclusion of the lesson, each student should:

1. Know the source of a fearful spirit.
2. Grasp how grace gives us confidence in God's love.
3. See how grace gives us access to God's power.
4. Understand how grace gives us the mind of Christ.
5. Be eagerly anticipating Jesus' return for His children.

Teaching Outline

I. His Grace Reassures Us with Power
  A. Power from the Holy Spirit
    1. The Holy Spirit resides in every born-again Christian.
    2. The Holy Spirit imparts grace and strength to a yielded Christian.
  B. Power for every Burden
    1. Power for witnessing
    2. Power in persecution

II. His Grace Reassures Us with Love
  A. A love for God
    1. We respond to His love.
    2. We reflect the spirit of His love.

B. A love for others

III. His Grace Reassures Us with a Sound Mind
   A. Through salvation
      1. Salvation is available through Jesus Christ.
      2. Salvation allows us the ability to understand spiritual things.
   B. Through the Scriptures
      1. The Scriptures give wisdom.
      2. The Scriptures produce a sound mind.
   C. Through the Second Coming of Jesus Christ

A Reassuring Grace

Text

2 TIMOTHY 1:5–9

5   When I call to remembrance the unfeigned faith that is in thee, which dwelt first in thy grandmother Lois, and thy mother Eunice; and I am persuaded that in thee also.

6   Wherefore I put thee in remembrance that thou stir up the gift of God, which is in thee by the putting on of my hands.

7   For God hath not given us the spirit of fear; but of power, and of love, and of a sound mind.

8   Be not thou therefore ashamed of the testimony of our Lord, nor of me his prisoner: but be thou partaker of the afflictions of the gospel according to the power of God;

9   Who hath saved us, and called us with an holy calling, not according to our works, but according to his own purpose and grace, which was given us in Christ Jesus before the world began,

Introduction

The first-century church faced great persecution. Because Christianity was not a socially acceptable religion, announcing you were a Christian could cost you your job, your family, and even your life. So it's not surprising that Paul's letters often start with the phrase, "Grace to you." These people needed God's grace, and so do we today.

With the battles we face from day to day, we must *"be strong in the grace that is in Christ Jesus"* (2 Timothy 2:1) on a daily basis. Receiving God's grace is not a one-time event; we need that grace continually. Timothy needed a special measure of grace for the ministry to which God had called him. Apart from the grace of God, we cannot effectively minister to anyone—whether by pastoring a church, teaching a Sunday school class, discipling a convert, working on a bus route, witnessing to the lost, or being a good spouse or parent. We need grace not only to grow personally but also to be a help and encouragement to others.

In our text, Paul draws a contrast between two spirits. One is the spirit of the world, which is characterized by fear. The other is the spirit of grace, which is characterized by power, love, and soundness of mind. Remember that 2 Timothy was Paul's last epistle. He wrote it from prison in Rome shortly before he was executed by Nero. Paul was not speaking about grace theoretically; he was speaking practically to both Timothy and himself—and to us. So let's look at how grace provides us reassurance, no matter what circumstances we may face.

I. His Grace Reassures Us with Power

Grace gives us God's power for our daily lives. As in so many other areas, the world offers substitutes for the power of

God. It's not uncommon to hear people talk about the power of positive thinking or the power of the human spirit. The U.S. Army uses the slogan "Be all that you can be." That is not enough! The power God offers us is not the power of humanistic philosophy; it is a divine power that only comes from Him. We need His power working first in us and then through us to accomplish His purposes in our lives.

A. Power from the Holy Spirit

Worry, fear, and doubt leave us worn down as we struggle through this life in our own feeble strength. God offers to replace our inadequate resources with His power. The Greek word for *power, dunamis,* refers to "strength or power that is inherent; that resides in someone or something by virtue of its nature." Our God is a God of power and might. Strength and power are inherent to His nature. In fact, one common name for Him in the Old Testament is Almighty God.

1. THE HOLY SPIRIT RESIDES IN EVERY BORN-AGAIN CHRISTIAN.

JOHN 3:6

6   *That which is born of the flesh is flesh; and that which is born of the Spirit is spirit.*

ROMANS 8:8–9

8   *So then they that are in the flesh cannot please God.*

9   *But ye are not in the flesh, but in the Spirit, if so be that the Spirit of God dwell in you. Now if any man have not the Spirit of Christ, he is none of his.*

At the moment you were saved, the Holy Spirit of God took up residence within you. His presence is settled and certain; He will never forsake or abandon you. With His constant presence, we have access to His power. Our will is not the source of our power; our thoughts are not the source of our power; He is the source of our power and strength, if we depend upon His strength rather than on our own.

2. THE HOLY SPIRIT IMPARTS GRACE AND STRENGTH TO A YIELDED CHRISTIAN.

LUKE 24:49

49 And, behold, I send the promise of my Father upon you: but tarry ye in the city of Jerusalem, until ye be endued with the power from on high.

1 THESSALONIANS 5:19

19 Quench not the Spirit.

The Holy Spirit is the third person of the Trinity; He is just that—a person. He has feelings, and we can grieve Him by the way we live; thus, through rebellion and disobedience, we can quench His work in our lives (Ephesians 4:30). It's important to realize that although the Holy Spirit is present, indwelling every believer, His grace works in our lives only as we are yielded to Him; He will not force grace upon us.

Illustration

I heard of a man who said his wife hadn't spoken to him in three days. He related the story this way: "I think it has something to do with what happened Sunday night. My wife nudged me and said, 'I heard a noise downstairs. I think there are burglars in the kitchen. It sounds like they're eating the pork casserole I made for supper.' 'That will teach them!' I told her." Some people have a knack for saying things that quench a person's spirit.

We desire God's strength to sustain us through our trials and difficulties. We desire His power working through us so that our lives make a difference. And He desires to supply the strength and power we long for. Why then do we struggle along without them? Examine your heart. Are you bitter? Are you rebellious? Are you stubbornly refusing to let go of a besetting sin? When we harbor sin or bitterness in our hearts, we quench the work of grace that the Holy Spirit wants to do for us.

In his book *How to Pray*, E. M. Bounds wrote, "We are constantly on a stretch, if not on a strain, to devise new methods, new plans, new organizations to advance the church and secure enlargement and efficiency for the gospel. This trend of the day has a tendency to lose sight of the man or sink the man in the plan or organization. God's plan is to make much of the man, far more of him than of anything else. Men are God's method. The church is looking for better methods; God is looking for better men.... What the church needs today is not more machinery or better, not new organizations or more and novel methods, but men whom the Holy Spirit can use— men of prayer, mighty in prayer. The Holy Spirit does not flow through methods, but through men. He does not come on machinery, but on men. He does not anoint plans, but men—men of prayer." God is interested in the man. What does He see when He looks at your heart and life?

B. *Power for every burden*

Timothy would face great burdens. His spiritual father, his friend, his mentor, the Apostle Paul, would soon be put to death. At this time, Timothy was still a relatively young man, and not everyone took him seriously as a spiritual leader. As a young man, he would have to confront false teaching and apostasy in the church—without Paul's help. He would face persecution himself. In fact, church history tells us that while Timothy was pastoring the church at Ephesus, he was martyred for his opposition to idolatry in that city. Timothy faced many burdens for which he needed God's power. It is no wonder that Paul wrote to him of grace.

1.   POWER FOR WITNESSING

1 THESSALONIANS 1:5

5   *For our gospel came not unto you in word only, but also in power, and in the Holy Ghost, and in much assurance; as ye know what manner of men we were among you for your sake.*

Most people have difficulty speaking to someone about the Gospel because it is not a natural thing to do. Evangelist Gypsy Smith said, "Anyone can preach to a crowd. It takes the grace of God to preach to one man." Sometimes when we go door-to-door soulwinning, we knock or ring the doorbell and hope that no one is home. And even if we know all the verses and have prepared a plan to present salvation, we still cannot win men to Christ in our power; winning men is the work of the Holy Spirit of God. Our witnessing will fail without His power that flows through a yielded life.

2. POWER IN PERSECUTION

The threat of persecution that Timothy faced was very real. Christians were suffering for their faith in Christ. Even today in many countries, open declarations of faith can be followed with severe consequences. Here in America, we have been blessed with freedom to worship and witness for more than two hundred years. As a result, most of us have never faced any serious consequences for our faith. We have no guarantee that will always be the case.

Though we are not facing active persecution, we do face many obstacles to doing right. Because of cultural pressure, many parents lower their standards to avoid fighting with their teenagers. The same pressure causes many churches to drop doctrinal positions they have held for years to accommodate more current practices. It is never God's will to change a standard that is based on the Scriptures. To stand firmly against opposition, we need the power of God.

COLOSSIANS 1:10–11

10 *That ye might walk worthy of the Lord unto all pleasing, being fruitful in every good work, and increasing in the knowledge of God;*
11 *Strengthened with all might, according to his glorious power, unto all patience and longsuffering with joyfulness;*

ROMANS 8:26

26 *Likewise the Spirit also helpeth our infirmities: for we know not what we should pray for as we ought: but the Spirit itself maketh intercession for us with groanings that cannot be uttered.*

When we go through trials, we should be willing to change anything God wants us to change. But we should also refuse to change the things that are right, even if doing so would seemingly make our lives easier. You will never face a trial or persecution that you cannot endure in the power of the Holy Spirit.

Illustration

The song "God Will Make a Way" expresses the great truth that "God will make a way where there seems to be no way." In telling the story behind that song, Don Moen, the author, expressed that he and his brother were very close, as were their children. One day in a tragic accident, a semi hit Don's brother's family van broadside. All four of Don's nephews were thrown from the vehicle, and the oldest was killed. In his pain and grief, he wrote the words of comfort and faith that have been a blessing to so many people. God's Spirit will be there for you in suffering and persecution to give you the power to prevail.

II. His Grace Reassures Us with Love

In the struggles and difficulties that we face, we need the reassurance of love. When a child falls down and scrapes a knee, what is the first reaction? "Kiss it, Mommy!" While a kiss won't heal a wound, it is the expression of love that gives hope to the hurting one. Grace comes when our hearts are hurting and reassures us with love.

A. A love for God

Grace provides us with a personal relationship with the love of God. This goes beyond the "Honk if you love Jesus" bumper sticker level. This is an experience of His love that brings us salvation, and fills our hearts with love for Him.

1.   WE RESPOND TO HIS LOVE.

1 JOHN 4:19

19   We love him, because he first loved us.

Our love for God is not something that we produce on our own; it is a reflection of and response to the love that He first lavished on us. We did not initiate our love for Him. In fact, the Bible tells us that we were enemies of God, yet He loved us. This gracious, sacrificial love cannot be measured or compared to any human standard. It is, as Charles Wesley wrote in his hymn, a "love divine, all loves excelling."

Illustration

I was preparing a message and searched a database for "the love of God" to get some information and detail. The computer hummed and whirred a few moments. Then a message popped up on the screen: "Your search inquiry returned too many results. Please refine your search." This message was a simple reminder that we have a God who loves us so much that we cannot begin to search the riches of His love.

2.   WE REFLECT THE SPIRIT OF HIS LOVE.

1 JOHN 4:18

18   There is no fear in love; but perfect love casteth out fear: because fear hath torment. He that feareth is not made perfect in love.

Once we have His love, we can reflect it to others. Love is not simply a feeling of affection for someone; it is actively working and sacrificing to make the other person's life better. It was God's love for us that sent Jesus to die for our sins. And it is a reflection of that love that motivates us to reach out with the Gospel to a lost and dying world.

Illustration

Pastor John Olores, who has pastored for a number of years in the Philippines, is an example of one who reflects the love of God. Several years ago he was riding on a bus when it was taken over by Muslim terrorists. After they had separated the passengers into Muslims and Christians, they shot and killed Pastor Olores's infant son. He pastors just a few minutes away from the spot where his son died. This Filipino pastor later returned to the very village that was home to many of those terrorists. The same hands that bore that dead infant knocked on door after door in that village, bringing the Gospel of Christ. The same heart that felt the grief of losing a son felt compassion for those who needed to hear the story of God's love. He is a demonstration of a life lived in the strength and power of the Holy Spirit.

B. A love for others

GALATIANS 5:22

22 *But the fruit of the Spirit is love…*

GALATIANS 5:25

25 *If we live in the Spirit, let us also walk in the Spirit.*

When we love God and we are walking in the Spirit, it is natural for us to love others. But in our flesh, it is easy to find reasons not to love. In loving others, there is a very real possibility of being hurt. Sometimes husbands or wives are afraid to fully love their spouse because of something that has happened in the past. But remember that the spirit of fear does not come from God. His Spirit gives you love for others.

Illustration

A little girl was learning the fruit of the Spirit for her Sunday school class, and her father was going to help by listening to her recite them. She started down the list: "Love, joy, peace, longsuffering, faithfulness, gentleness and…uh…remote control!" She didn't have it quite right. What about you? Are you walking in the Spirit? Are your actions and reactions to others controlled by Him? Are you reflecting and expressing God's love to others?

III. His Grace Reassures Us with a Sound Mind

A sound mind is a mind that is well balanced, a mind that is under sound influences. There are many forces in the world striving to influence and control your mind. The devil knows that if he can control your thinking, he will eventually be able to control your conduct. The Holy Spirit works in the lives of yielded Christians to control their minds for good and righteous living.

A. Through salvation

This is a basic, foundational truth—you will never have a sound mind until your salvation is settled. Where the devil offers doubt and fear, God offers certainty. You can indeed know for sure that you are saved, that your eternal destiny is settled. You can be confident because the promises of God are immutable, settled and secure.

1. SALVATION IS AVAILABLE THROUGH JESUS CHRIST.

TITUS 3:4–7

4 But after that the kindness and love of God our Saviour toward man appeared,

5 Not by works of righteousness which we have done, but according to his mercy he saved us, by the washing of regeneration, and renewing of the Holy Ghost;

6 Which he shed on us abundantly through Jesus Christ our Saviour;

7 That being justified by his grace, we should be made heirs according to the hope of eternal life.

Many people think they are saved, and if you ask them, they will say that they are. In fact one recent poll showed that seventy-six percent of American adults claimed to be Christians! The truth is that most of these people have never had a specific time when they accepted Christ as Saviour. They may have a cultural religion, but they do not have a personal relationship with Jesus. It is not our profession of salvation but our possession of salvation that gives us a sound mind.

2. SALVATION ALLOWS US THE ABILITY TO UNDERSTAND SPIRITUAL THINGS.

1 CORINTHIANS 2:14

14 But the natural man receiveth not the things of the Spirit of God: for they are foolishness unto him: neither can he know them, because they are spiritually discerned.

"I don't understand how God could…" commonly launches the argument made by those who insist the Bible doesn't make sense. Well, of course they don't understand. To a lost person, the Bible is a false and foolish collection of folk tales made up to control weak-minded people. Because it is a spiritual book, it can only be understood through the indwelling Holy Spirit of God. He teaches us the purpose and meaning of the words that He inspired for our instruction.

> **TEACHING TIP**
>
> *Do not make the assumption that all of the members of your class are saved. People come to church for many reasons, and their presence does not guarantee that they have personally experienced salvation. This is a good place to review God's plan of salvation, and how we can receive it. You may want to ask some of your class members to give a testimony of their salvation. And before this lesson ends, offer private help to anyone who is unsure of whether he is saved. Also observe each member to see if there are any responses that might suggest someone is uncertain. You should follow up with him even if he does not come to you for help.*

B. *Through the Scriptures*

The teaching of the Word of God is the foundation for sound minds. The philosophies and opinions of men constantly change. But the Word of God is settled in Heaven forever, eternally accurate and unchanging (Psalm 119:89). There is no other foundation on which you can develop a settled mind.

1. THE SCRIPTURES GIVE WISDOM.

2 TIMOTHY 3:15

15 And that from a child thou hast known the holy scriptures, which are able to make thee wise unto salvation through faith which is in Christ Jesus.

PROVERBS 1:7

7 The fear of the LORD is the beginning of knowledge: but fools despise wisdom and instruction.

Through His Word, we understand how God wants us to live. Knowing the Bible requires careful study. D.L. Moody said, "I am glad there are things in the Bible I do not understand. If I could take that book up and read it as I would any other book, I might think I could write a book like that." But as believers we have the Holy Spirit to help us understand the teachings of the Scriptures.

2. THE SCRIPTURES PRODUCE A SOUND MIND.

2 TIMOTHY 3:16–17

16 All scripture is given by inspiration of God, and is profitable for doctrine, for reproof, for correction, for instruction in righteousness:
17 That the man of God may be perfect, throughly furnished unto all good works.

Our human reasoning isn't enough to allow us to discern truth from error with confidence. The best protection against deceptive thoughts and attitudes is to know God's revealed truth, the Bible. The more Bible you know and put into practice, the more settled your mind will be. The instruction that you need, everything required for godly living (2 Peter 1:3) is available to you within the pages of God's Word.

C. Through the Second Coming of Jesus Christ

1 Thessalonians 4:13–18

13   But I would not have you to be ignorant, brethren, concerning them which are asleep, that ye sorrow not, even as others which have no hope.

14   For if we believe that Jesus died and rose again, even so them also which sleep in Jesus will God bring with him.

15   For this we say unto you by the word of the Lord, that we which are alive and remain unto the coming of the Lord shall not prevent them which are asleep.

16   For the Lord himself shall descend from heaven with a shout, with the voice of the archangel, and with the trump of God: and the dead in Christ shall rise first.

17   Then we which are alive and remain shall be caught up together with them in the clouds, to meet the Lord in the air: and so shall we ever be with the Lord.

18   Wherefore comfort one another with these words.

Things happen in this world that we don't understand. Why do bad things happen to good people? Why do Sunday school teachers get cancer while evil men lead healthy lives? Why do we have so many troubles and trials? Those questions will engender unsoundness in our minds unless we realize one central truth: Jesus is coming back to settle all accounts. This world is not all there is. We have the comfort of a reunion with Him in our future. All wrongs will be righted in that day. God is always in control.

Conclusion

Paul told Timothy that we are called *"according to his purpose and grace."* God has a plan and a purpose for your life. He is not surprised by anything that happens to you. He is never caught off guard, and He never makes a mistake. Difficulties are going to come into our lives that we do not understand. In this life, we may never understand why. But we can trust in His love and goodness that it is all according to His plan.

God wants to give you grace to live in power and love with a sound mind. The choice is up to you. Will you yield to His Spirit that you might experience His power? Will you grow in grace, allowing your confidence in Him to overcome your doubts? Will you place your hand in His and allow Him to lead your every step on the path that He planned for you to walk?

Study Questions

1. How does God's grace reassure us with power?
   He gives us power through the Holy Spirit and power for every burden.

2. How has God empowered you to be an effective witness for Him?
   Answers will vary.

3. How does God's grace reassure us with love?
   A love for God; a love for others

4. What are we doing when we show love to others?
   Reflecting God's love

5. What does it mean to have a sound mind?
   A well-balanced mind

6. What fears can keep you from having a sound mind?
   Answers will vary.

7. How does God's grace reassure us with a sound mind?
   Through salvation, through the Scriptures, through the Second Coming

8. How were we called to be God's children?
   According to His purpose and grace

Memory Verses

COLOSSIANS 1:10–11

10 That ye might walk worthy of the Lord unto all pleasing, being fruitful in every good work, and increasing in the knowledge of God;

11 Strengthened with all might, according to his glorious power, unto all patience and longsuffering with joyfulness.

A Reinforcing Grace

Text

ROMANS 5:1–5

1   Therefore being justified by faith, we have peace with God through our Lord Jesus Christ:

2   By whom also we have access by faith into this grace wherein we stand, and rejoice in hope of the glory of God.

3   And not only so, but we glory in tribulations also: knowing that tribulation worketh patience;

4   And patience, experience; and experience, hope:

5   And hope maketh not ashamed; because the love of God is shed abroad in our hearts by the Holy Ghost which is given unto us.

Overview

When a general is planning a battle, one of his most important strategies is positioning his troops so there will be reinforcements available if something goes wrong in one area of the battle. If he cannot provide help at the crucial moment, the entire battle may be lost.

The Christian life is a life of spiritual warfare. We are wrestling in a life-and-death struggle against a very real enemy committed to our destruction. But we have reinforcements available to us. Grace provides the help we need to fight and win the battles we face. In this lesson we're going to study how grace supplies what we lack in the areas of unity, stability, and maturity. With these missing elements supplied, we are prepared for every attack of the enemy.

Lesson Aim

We want the students to be focused on fighting and winning their spiritual battles, not in their own strength, but in the power and grace of God.

Lesson Goals

At the conclusion of the lesson, each student should:

1. Have a full appreciation for the seriousness of the spiritual battle he faces.
2. Know the basis and reason for unity in the body of Christ.
3. See the need for stability at home, at church, and at work.
4. Appreciate the process by which God brings us to spiritual maturity.
5. Be equipped to help and encourage others as they labor together for the Lord.

Teaching Outline

I. A Grace that Brings Unity
   A. Unity comes through justification.
      1. The meaning of justification
      2. The message of justification
   B. Justification is the gift of the Lord Jesus.
      1. He satisfied God's just demands.
      2. He reconciled man to God.

II. A Grace that Brings Stability
   A. His grace is accessible.
   B. His grace is stabilizing.

C.   His grace brings hope.

III. A Grace that Brings Maturity
    A.   Maturity through tribulations
    B.   Maturity to bring patience
    C.   Maturity through experience
    D.   Maturity to hope

A Reinforcing Grace

Text

ROMANS 5:1–5

1   Therefore being justified by faith, we have peace with God through our Lord Jesus Christ:

2   By whom also we have access by faith into this grace wherein we stand, and rejoice in hope of the glory of God.

3   And not only so, but we glory in tribulations also: knowing that tribulation worketh patience;

4   And patience, experience; and experience, hope:

5   And hope maketh not ashamed; because the love of God is shed abroad in our hearts by the Holy Ghost which is given unto us.

Introduction

On January 31, 2000, Alaska Airlines Flight 261 left Puerto Vallarta, Mexico en route to San Francisco with eighty-eight passengers and crew on board. At 28,000 feet above the Pacific Ocean near Catalina Island, the crew reported problems with the plane's stabilizer trim. These small flaps on the horizontal portion of the tail control the pitch of the aircraft. In just a few moments, the plane started an uncontrolled descent into the ocean, killing everyone on board.

In their investigation, the National Transportation Safety Board discovered that the jackscrew, which helped control the stabilizer trim, had not been maintained properly. Because the jackscrew had not been greased, it was unable to move, causing the catastrophic crash. This tiny piece of a gigantic aircraft determined the fate of everyone on board.

Too often we are tempted to neglect the small, hidden areas of the Christian life, and as a result, disaster ensues. One of those hidden areas is growing in grace. From the outside it is nearly impossible to tell if you have shrugged off your spiritual maintenance for a day or two. But continually neglecting the spiritual needs of your heart will eventually have devastating results. To prevent tragedy, let's learn how God's grace will bring unity, stability, and maturity to our lives.

I.   A Grace That Brings Unity

The most important kind of unity that exists is our unity with God through Christ. Only through His grace can we find peace with God and enter into a relationship of harmony with Him. The only real and lasting basis we have for our unity as believers is the shared justification we have all received through His grace. We need unity in our homes, at our work, and in our churches. That unity comes through the grace of God.

A. Unity comes through justification.

ROMANS 3:23

23   For all have sinned, and come short of the glory of God.

No church or institution, no pastor or priest, no set of good works can impart to you unity with God. Because God is just and holy, He cannot have fellowship with us in our sinful state. So that we could be reunited with God, Jesus shed His blood to cover our sin, justifying us and bringing us into unity with God.

1.   THE MEANING OF JUSTIFICATION

The Greek word for *justification* is *dikaioo* meaning "to declare or pronounce one to be just, righteous; to declare the sinner righteous." Warren Wiersbe said, "Justification is God's declaration that the believing sinner is righteous in Christ. It is righteousness imputed, put to our account." When we received Christ as Saviour, the blood He shed on the Cross was applied to our account, and we, though we were dirty and wretched and blind, were declared righteous.

When a sinner is justified, he is at peace with God. And because he has peace *with* God, he can have the peace *of* God.

2.   THE MESSAGE OF JUSTIFICATION

ROMANS 5:10

10   For if, when we were enemies, we were reconciled to God by the death of his Son, we shall be saved by his life.

We were God's enemies before we received His grace, but when God justified us, He brought us into the close fellowship He shares with Jesus (1 John 1:3). The unity we have now is the same kind that Adam and Eve enjoyed with God before sin entered into the world. Justification means that God treats us just as if we had never sinned. Justification is a message of hope and reconciliation, and it is only possible through Jesus Christ.

B. Justification is the gift of the Lord Jesus.

Have you ever received a really expensive gift? Maybe your parents or your spouse saved money for a long time to get you something special that you really wanted. How did you feel when you got that gift? Have you ever forgotten it? The best gift you have or will ever receive pales in comparison to your justification. What did we receive with our justification?

1. HE SATISFIED GOD'S JUST DEMANDS.
ROMANS 3:24–26

24 Being justified freely by his grace through the redemption that is in Christ Jesus:

25 Whom God hath set forth to be a propitiation through faith in his blood, to declare his righteousness for the remission of sins that are past, through the forbearance of God;

26 To declare, I say, at this time his righteousness: that he might be just, and the justifier of him which believeth in Jesus.

We must never forget the sacrifice the Lord Jesus made to satisfy God's holiness and righteousness on our behalf. Christ's death allowed God to forgive the sinner and to accept him as righteous in His eyes. There is no other way that we could ever stand before Him. Yet so many people think that they are going to slip through a loophole somehow or that their good works will outweigh their bad deeds and they will get into Heaven.

There is no other way to the Father except through Jesus (John 14:6), for no one else could offer the sinless sacrifice that satisfied the demand of a holy God for justice. It would be more politically correct to say there are other ways to Heaven, but we declare the exclusivity of Jesus as the only Justifier for man.

Illustration

During an edition of the news program *60 Minutes*, Dan Rather interviewed Jack Welch, the outspoken former CEO of General Electric. At the end of the interview, Rather asked Welch, "What's the toughest question you have ever been asked?" Welch replied, "Do you think you'll go to Heaven?" When asked how he answered, Welch continued, "It's a long answer, but I said that if caring about people, if giving it your all, if being a great friend counts—despite the fact that I've been divorced a couple of times, and no one's proud of that; I haven't done everything right all the time—I think I've got a shot at Heaven. I'm in no hurry to get there and to find out any time soon."

The truth is, we can know that we will go to Heaven, but this assurance is not based on our good works; it is based on trusting in Jesus Christ alone (1 John 5:13).

2. HE RECONCILED MAN TO GOD.
EPHESIANS 1:6–7
6   *To the praise of the glory of his grace, wherein he hath made us accepted in the beloved.*
7   *In whom we have redemption through his blood, the forgiveness of sins, according to the riches of his grace;*

When sin separated man from God, Adam and Eve were driven out of the Garden of Eden, losing the daily fellowship they had once enjoyed. From that day forward, because of sin, man was an enemy of God. Now through reconciliation by Jesus' sacrifice we have been brought back into the union of fellowship with the Heavenly Father.

EPHESIANS 2:15–16

15 Having abolished in his flesh the enmity, even the law of commandments contained in ordinances; for to make in himself of twain one new man, so making peace;

16 And that he might reconcile both unto God in one body by the cross, having slain the enmity thereby:

II. A Grace That Brings Stability

1 PETER 5:10–11

10 But the God of all grace, who hath called us unto his eternal glory by Christ Jesus, after that ye have suffered a while, make you perfect, stablish, strengthen, settle you.

11 To him be glory and dominion for ever and ever. Amen.

No matter what is happening in our lives, grace can give us stability. The people to whom Peter wrote were undergoing incredible persecution and struggles. Yet he said that they could be established by the God of all grace. You do not have to live with uncertainty and doubt. You can be settled and confident in His love for you.

A. His grace is accessible.

In the days of the tabernacle and the Temple, no one was allowed into the Holy of Holies, except for the

High Priest on the Day of Atonement. The way into the glory of God's presence was disallowed because of sin. When Christ died on the Cross, having satisfied God's demands for justice, He *"rent in twain"* the Temple veil that represents our separation from God, making access to God obtainable by grace through faith. The access that Paul spoke of in our text is *prosagoge* in the Greek, which means "approach as to God, i.e., that relationship with God whereby we are acceptable to Him and have assurance that He is favorably disposed towards us." Because of grace, God is now approachable. For any relationship to be stable, the individuals in that relationship must be approachable. Our Heavenly Father is approachable because of our new relationship in Jesus Christ. Before our salvation, we stood condemned "in Adam," but "in Christ," we stand perfect before God who invites us to come boldly into His presence. No one must go to God for us; as believer-priests, we have complete access to Him ourselves.

Illustration

When I was growing up, the Oakland A's were the best baseball team around. They won three consecutive World Series titles from 1972–1974. I remember watching Rollie Fingers, Reggie Jackson, Sal Bando, Catfish Hunter and the other great players who made them an unstoppable team. I got to go to a few games, but we had to sit way up in the outfield bleachers.

Then one day, Alvin Dark, the manager of the Oakland A's, joined the church we attended. He had been an outstanding baseball player and would go on to win nearly 1,000 games as a manager. When he got to know our family, he gave my father passes to take us to the 1974

World Series between the Oakland A's and the Dodgers. That was an amazing day in my life. We went in through a special entrance to our seats right on the first baseline, and my brother and I even got autographs from Reggie Jackson. We were living every kid's dream! Why? Because a man who had a position with the team gave us access. In the same way, Jesus gives us access to God's riches.

HEBREWS 10:19–23

19 Having therefore, brethren, boldness to enter into the holiest by the blood of Jesus,

20 By a new and living way, which he hath consecrated for us, through the veil, that is to say, his flesh;

21 And having an high priest over the house of God;

22 Let us draw near with a true heart in full assurance of faith, having our hearts sprinkled from an evil conscience, and our bodies washed with pure water.

23 Let us hold fast the profession of our faith without wavering; (for he is faithful that promised;)

HEBREWS 4:14–16

14 Seeing then that we have a great high priest, that is passed into the heavens, Jesus the Son of God, let us hold fast our profession.

15 For we have not an high priest which cannot be touched with the feeling of our infirmities; but was in all points tempted like as we are, yet without sin.

16 Let us therefore come boldly unto the throne of grace, that we may obtain mercy, and find grace to help in time of need.

B. His grace is stabilizing.

Grace gives us this new standing before God. Paul described it as *"the grace wherein we stand."* We never have to fear or wonder regarding God's love and care for us. It is settled through grace. In a world of worry and doubt, we can be fully confident, because our standing is not based on anything we have done; it is based solely on the grace we have through Jesus Christ.

Illustration

One of the most famous scientists of the ancient world was Archimedes of Syracuse, a mathematician, astronomer, engineer, and inventor. Several of his inventions are still in use today. One of his most famous sayings was, "Give me a lever long enough and a place on which to stand and I can move the world." One of the most important things about grace is that it gives us a solid and certain place on which to stand.

C. His grace brings hope.

There is no stability in a life that has no hope. One who has doubts and questions about his eternal soul will never find true peace in his life, nor will he experience stability. He needs hope—a confident and joyful expectation of eternal salvation. As a Christian, you have that certain hope. Your destiny is settled and secure. Nothing can take God's grace away from you.

TITUS 3:5–7

5   *Not by works of righteousness which we have done, but according to his mercy he saved us, by the washing of regeneration, and renewing of the Holy Ghost;*

6   *Which he shed on us abundantly through Jesus Christ our Saviour;*

7   *That being justified by his grace, we should be made heirs according to the hope of eternal life.*

1 PETER 1:3–4

3   Blessed be the God and Father of our Lord Jesus Christ, which according to his abundant mercy hath begotten us again unto a lively hope by the resurrection of Jesus Christ from the dead,

4   To an inheritance incorruptible, and undefiled, and that fadeth not away, reserved in heaven for you,

Most of the people I know are not going to receive a huge inheritance. Maybe you have a rich uncle somewhere who is going to remember you in his will, but that is the exception instead of the rule. But Paul told Titus that we have been made heirs with Jesus, which means that we are entitled to share with Him everything that He has. What could be a better source of hope than that?

Paul said in Romans 5:2 that we can *"rejoice in hope of the glory of God."* This statement puts in a nutshell what salvation and eternal security is all about—the confidence that when you have been saved, it is "for keeps." Perhaps the greatest declaration in all of Scripture regarding the certainty of God's love is found in Romans 8.

ROMANS 8:31–39

31   What shall we then say to these things? If God be for us, who can be against us?

32   He that spared not his own Son, but delivered him up for us all, how shall he not with him also freely give us all things?

33   Who shall lay anything to the charge of God's elect? It is God that justifieth.

34   Who is he that condemneth? It is Christ that died, yea rather, that is risen again, who is even at the right hand of God, who also maketh intercession for us.

35 *Who shall separate us from the love of Christ? shall tribulation, or distress, or persecution, or famine, or nakedness, or peril, or sword?*

36 *As it is written, For thy sake we are killed all the day long; we are accounted as sheep for the slaughter.*

37 *Nay, in all these things we are more than conquerors through him that loved us.*

38 *For I am persuaded, that neither death, nor life, nor angels, nor principalities, nor powers, nor things present, nor things to come,*

39 *Nor height, nor depth, nor any other creature, shall be able to separate us from the love of God, which is in Christ Jesus our Lord.*

TEACHING TIP

The concept of an inheritance is something your students will understand. A good way to start the conversation is to mention something that you received—perhaps a family heirloom, a piece of furniture, or a picture—from someone in your family. Ask the students to share their stories as well. Talk about the fact that what you inherit is determined by what the testator possessed. Then share with them from the Scriptures (Psalm 24:1; Philippians 4:19) the incredible riches of God, and remind them that this is what we have to anticipate!

III. A Grace That Brings Maturity

We often talk about "growing in grace." What does that phrase mean exactly? It is referring to the process by which we mature as believers. Just as our physical bodies grow and become stronger after we are born, our spiritual life needs to develop as well. Do not settle for your current level of growth. God has something better in mind for you.

Every gardener who invests in a garden expects the plants to grow. If a plant does not mature or grow, the gardener is unable to enjoy the fruits of his labor. It's sad to see a garden that has shriveled and withered—just as it's sad to see a Christian who has failed to grow in grace that he might bring forth fruit for God.

God's design for our lives is that we will be firmly rooted in His grace so that we grow to maturity. He does not want us to be easily swayed or wilt when troubles come. Romans 5 lays out for us four ways that maturity develops in our lives.

A. Maturity through tribulations

How is it possible to "glory in tribulations"? Most of the time we fret or despair when trouble comes instead of rejoicing. We must understand that the trials that come into our lives are for a specific purpose—to produce patience. Grace is not just for the mountaintop; through grace we can rejoice even in the valley.

The word *tribulation* comes to us from the Latin *tribulum* which means "a heavy instrument used to process grain." The *tribulum* had a heavy stone cylinder with sharp rocks and bits of iron embedded in it. As it was dragged over the grain, it would tear the chaff away. That is what tribulations do for us—they remove the chaff from our lives and leave behind that which is worthwhile and useful in our service to the Lord.

Notice also that the Bible says *"tribulation worketh patience."* This is not an immediate process. The word *worketh* means "to perform, accomplish, achieve; to work out—i.e., to do that from which something results." The reason grace enables us to rejoice in tribulation is that we know trials bring God's desired intent. When we understand there is purpose in a trial, we respond to it differently according to the grace that we have received from God.

B. Maturity to bring patience

JAMES 1:2–4

2 *My brethren, count it all joy when ye fall into divers temptations;*

3 *Knowing this, that the trying of your faith worketh patience.*

4 *But let patience have her perfect work, that ye may be perfect and entire, wanting nothing.*

Tribulations bring patience into our lives, but that is just the beginning of the process that God has designed for us. Patience also has work to do in our lives; it makes us complete—lacking nothing we need to accomplish God's predestined purposes. I remember a man saying to me once, "I've tithed seven weeks in a row, and now I've lost my job. That giving stuff doesn't work!" Don't get discouraged with the work God is doing in your life; He hasn't finished yet.

Second only to suffering, waiting may be the greatest teacher of godliness, maturity, and genuine spirituality. Long afflictions borne patiently show a Christian what he is made of; they test his religion and prove that it is genuine. God does not test us to make us quit; He tests us so that we can gain the experience we need to achieve maturity. And if you quit, you will miss out on what He wants to do in your life.

C. Maturity through experience

Experience results from the process of proving. The Greek word for *experience* is *dokimeen,* which means "a trial, or testing." God's plan for our lives is not instant gratification. Full-grown oak trees are not produced in three years; neither are servants of God. When you see a big, beautiful oak tree, you are probably looking at a seventy or eighty-year-old tree. It is the product of a long process of growth. So it must be with a fully developed Christian.

God's plan is a complete cycle. It starts and ends with hope.

We started with the "hope of the glory of God"
…then rejoicing in tribulations
…then tribulation working patience
…which then produces stability
…steadfastness produces experience
…which produces hope!

D. Maturity to hope

As we grow in grace, we learn to hope, no matter how difficult the circumstances may seem. The kind of hope that God offers is dependable hope. Paul tells us it is hope that *"maketh not ashamed"*—that is, it doesn't result in disappointment.

Paul talks about God's love being *"shed abroad in our hearts"* through grace. This is not talking about a small measure; the phrase means to "pour out." There is no shortage of grace. God has more than enough to last your entire life and to meet your every need.

Illustration

At seventy-three years of age, John Wesley related in his journal (June 28, 1776) that he was far more able to preach than he had been when he was twenty-three years old. Rising each day at four in the morning to pray, he traveled more than 4,000 miles a year (giving him exercise and "change of air"). He was able to go to sleep immediately at night, never losing a night's sleep in his entire life. Even with his rigorous schedule, he experienced only four illnesses that were "used to invigorate him." He wrote about possessing "evenness of temper" as he testified of God's grace: "I feel and grieve, but by the grace of God, I fret at nothing."

Conclusion

Everything that happens in our lives happens according to the design and purpose of God. Whether you have been saved for a few days or a few decades, God is working everything together—even things that from a human perspective seem "bad"—to make you more like His Son. It is grace that enables us to endure trials and tribulations that they may accomplish their intended results—building patience, experience, and hope into our lives.

Grace brings us into unity and fellowship with other believers because of our oneness with God the Father and Jesus Christ. Grace will give you stability and a firm foundation on which to stand. Grace will give you maturity as it empowers you to grow in Him. All of these gifts of grace are freely offered to us, but not every Christian benefits from the full measure of God's grace. That is not God's failure, or a lack of His grace; it is our failure to claim the inheritance that has been promised to us.

Grace is unfailing. I ask you this question: Will you still be faithful to God a year, five years, ten years from now? If you continue to grow in the grace of God, you will. Grace will keep you from becoming bitter or discouraged and throwing in the towel. Living in the grace of God will keep you on track and prevent you from becoming a shipwreck.

Study Questions

1. How does grace work to bring us unity?
    Unity comes through justification; justification is the gift of the Lord Jesus.

2. What did Jesus do for us on the Cross?
    He satisfied God's just demands; He reconciled man to God.

3. How has grace produced unity in your life?
    Answers will vary.

4. How does grace bring stability to our lives?
    His grace is accessible; His grace is stabilizing; His grace brings hope.

5. What is something that you hoped for in the past that God made a reality for you?
    Answers will vary.

6. What is something you are trusting and hoping for God to do in your life?
    Answers will vary.

7. In what four ways does grace produce maturity in our lives?
    Maturity through tribulation; maturity to bring patience; maturity through experience; maturity to hope

8. What is the biblical meaning of hope?
    Something that doesn't make us ashamed or disappoint us

Memory Verses
HEBREWS 4:14–16

14 Seeing then that we have a great high priest, that is passed into the heavens, Jesus the Son of God, let us hold fast our profession.

15 For we have not an high priest which cannot be touched with the feeling of our infirmities; but was in all points tempted like as we are, yet without sin.

16 Let us therefore come boldly unto the throne of grace, that we may obtain mercy, and find grace to help in time of need.

For additional Christian
growth resources visit
www.strivingtogether.com